ESCAPE
FROM
THE COMING
TRIBULATION

ESCAPE FROM THE COMING TRIBULATION

How to Be Prepared
for the Last Great Crisis of History

Guy Duty

BETHANY FELLOWSHIP, INC.
Minneapolis, Minnesota

Published by Bethany Fellowship, Inc.
6820 Auto Club Road, Minneapolis, Minnesota 55438

Printed in the United States of America

Library of Congress CIP Data:

Duty, Guy, 1907-
    Escape from the coming tribulation.

    Bibliography: p.
    1. Tribulation (Christian eschatology) I. Title.
BT888.D87   236'.3   75-17979
ISBN 0-87123-131-X

*Dedicated to
Arthur E. Bloomfield,
prophecy teacher extraordinary,
from whom I learned much*

Contents

CHAPTER 1

Statement of Purpose

During the past generation there has been a revival of interest in the biblical doctrine of Christ's second coming. And like other doctrines, there has been much controversy among teachers about the meaning of various scriptures that deal with His coming. One of the most disputed questions today is: "Will the Church go through the tribulation?"

The literature on this subject is abundant and confusing to the average reader. Peter wrote, "We have also a more sure word of prophecy; whereunto ye do well that ye take heed, as unto a light that shineth in a dark place, until the day dawn, and the day star arise in your hearts." God has given us a sure word of prophecy to shine in the present darkness and to guide us in times of perplexity and deception.

But we cannot have a sure word of prophecy unless we have a sure method of interpretation. The conflicts and differences between teachers of prophecy are due mainly to the differences in their methods of interpretation.

Paul told us to "prove all things," and nothing

is more important to prove than our doctrines. But how are we to prove them? We certainly cannot do it if each interpreter is allowed to have his own ideas about what the Scriptures mean. Rules of interpretation are necessary. Jesus and the apostles used established rules of interpretation to refute their opponents.

At the end of this book we have included nine rules which the reader should read carefully before he proceeds. These rules have been universally accepted by the countries of the free world where they are used in courts of evidence as bases of proof. No fair interpreter will refuse to accept them. Biblical language does not change, and we must judge it by the same laws that apply to other books.

Dean Farrar spent twenty years on his masterly work, *History of Interpretation*, in which he wrote about the distortions and errors of interpreters. He concluded that "the misinterpretation of Scripture must be reckoned among the gravest calamities of Christendom" (p. 39).

Will the Church go through the tribulation? Teachers on this question fall into three classes.

(1) Those who claim there will be a pretribulation translation (rapture) of the Church before the tribulation begins. They hold that the true Church will be caught away to be with the Lord during the entire tribulation period. These are called "Pre-tribulationists."

(2) Others contend that the Church must endure the first part of the tribulation, and that the translation or rapture of the Church will be at the middle of the tribulation. These are called "Mid-tribulationists."

(3) The third class believe that the Church must pass through the entire period of tribulation and that it will be translated at the end, which is the time of the Second Coming of Christ. These are known as "Post-tribulationists."

In presenting our case of escape from the tribulation, it will be seen from various texts that we distinguish between the Church *before* the tribulation begins and *after* it begins. This before-and-after point is important.

Jesus specified events that occurred in the days before the Flood: "For as in the days that were *before* the flood . . . ," so also shall it be before His coming (Matt. 24:37-38). Our case then will deal much with events that precede the beginning of the tribulation.

The question naturally arises: "Well, if the Church escapes the tribulation, *how* will it escape?" But it shall be our purpose only to show that it will escape, not how. We shall see later that Peter said, "The Lord knoweth *how* to deliver the godly out of temptation" (judgment), as He knew how to deliver Noah and Lot out of judgment (2 Pet. 2:9). God has not yet revealed all His secrets.

World events have brought a revival of interest in biblical prophecy; but, as always, sensationalists have appeared who stir up people with excitement and speculation. The Lord has not left this subject in obscurity, and people would be wise to avoid the emotional guesswork by calmly studying the Scriptures.

The texts are quoted from the King James Version except where otherwise specified. We acknowledge our appreciation to various copyright owners who kindly gave us permission to quote from their sources. News items were gathered from various sources, especially from the *U.S. News & World Report*.

The italics in Bible quotations represent my emphasis; they do not represent words that the original translators supplied to complete the meaning.

CHAPTER 2

Definition of Terms

Our Lord's most important prophetic message is generally considered to be the Olivet Discourse, found in Matthew 24:1-51, Mark 13:1-37, and Luke 21:5-36.

Jesus had a marvelous ability to sum up His purpose in a discourse with one or two sentences at the end, and Luke 21:34-36 is an example of this.

> And take heed to yourselves, lest at any time your hearts be overcharged with surfeiting, and drunkenness, and cares of this life, and so *that day* come upon you unawares.
>
> For as a *snare* shall it come on all them that dwell on the face of the whole earth.
>
> Watch ye therefore, and pray always, that ye may be accounted worthy to *escape* all these things that shall come to pass, and to stand before the Son of man.

Jesus here, as on other occasions, sounded a warning to the Church about the particular *dangers* at the end of the age. There have always been dangerous times for the Church, but those of the end time will be special and crucial—such as no other generation ever saw. For example, Satan has always set snares for the Church, but at no time in history has the Church seen the snare that Jesus warned about here. At no time did the Church see the approach of "that day" as we see it today.

No one was ever more precise with the use of words than was Jesus, and in the above verses He used three important terms: *that day*, *snare*, and *escape*. What did the greatest of teachers intend to convey to our minds with His use of these words? We must first get the definitions of these terms because we cannot know what He meant until we know the biblical meanings. As R. B. Girdlestone has well said in his book, *The Grammar of Prophecy*, "There is no royal road to the scientific study of prophecy. We have to begin with words and sentences before we launch into ideas" (p. 104).

The Jews were familiar with the term *that day* because it appears frequently in the Old Testament relating to the tribulation judgments. Similar terms also appear in the prophets. We often see the terms *day of wrath*, *the day*, *day of God*, *day of judgment*, *the great day*, and others. Their precise meaning is determined by the contexts in which they appear.

In the prophets, *that day* is a "day of judgment," and the *day of judgment* is the "day of God," and *day of God* is a "day of wrath," and so on. Often in the Old Testament, *day* and *days* are connected with judgment and are synonyms for judgment.

Isaiah says, "In that day . . . the Lord shall punish . . . the kings of the earth" (24:21). And Zephaniah says, "That day is a day of wrath, a day of trouble and distress" (1:15). Joel wrote about "the great and terrible day of the Lord" (2:31). The prophet Amos described the day of the Lord with the distinct detail of "a day of darkness" (5:18-20). According to Amos, the main characteristic of this period is darkness. Paul's use of the word agrees with this (1 Thess. 5:5-9).

That day is a chief prophetic term in both Testaments. It will be a period of tribulation for the whole earth. It will have a beginning—"the beginning of sorrows"; and it will have an end—"and then shall the end come" (Matt. 24:8, 14).

After a thorough study of *that day* and similar terms, we conclude that there is little difficulty in deciding their meanings. When the various uses of these terms are considered, it is clear that they can have a general or specific sense according to the contexts in which they appear.

We now consider the definition of *snare*. From standard sources we quote the following:

> "Snare (*pagis*), a trap to ensnare, is used metaphorically of the allurements to evil by which Satan ensnares one, 1 Tim. 3:7; 2 Tim. 2:26." It is also used "of the sudden judgments of God to come upon those whose hearts are 'overcharged with surfeiting, and drunkenness, and cares of this life,' Luke 21:34."[1]

> Snare (pagis) . . . it was a noose of hair for small birds, of wire for larger birds and animals. The snares were set in a favorable location and grain scattered to attract the attention of feathered creatures. They accepted the bribe of good feeding and walked into the snare, not suspecting danger. For this reason the snare became particularly applicable in describing a tempting bribe offered to men to lead their fellows into trouble.[2]

> Snare (pagis), a trap which holds fast . . . in which birds are entangled and caught . . . *unexpectedly, suddenly*, because birds and beasts are caught unawares, Luke 21:35. *A snare*, i.e., whatever

brings peril, loss, destruction: of a sudden and deadly peril.[3]

Isaiah 42:22 shows that a concealed hole in the ground was a snare. Jeremiah 18:22 indicates that the digging of a pit was a common device to ensnare. Amos 3:5 mentions a gin, which was a trap springing up from the ground to catch birds by the feet. Other traps caught animals by the neck.

Solomon warned us about the snares of love. And we learn from 1 Samuel 18:21 that women were used to ensnare men. Nations throughout history have often used this trap to steal military secrets.

Paul warned us that the love of money is a snare (1 Tim. 6:9). And the "cares [anxieties] of this life" are snares to many professing Christians. The snare of drugs is one of the worst. The list of snares is indeed a long one.

The word "escape" is *ekpheugo* in the Greek New Testament. It signifies "to get free from, to flee out of, to evade a captor, to get safely away from danger."

This can be verified from standard sources which also specify escape from the tribulation of Luke 21:36.[4]

Three examples of this definition will illustrate it. In Psalm 124:7, we read:

Our soul is escaped as a bird out of the snare of the fowlers: the snare is broken, and we are escaped.

In Psalm 141:9-10:

Keep me from the snares which they have laid for me, and the gins [traps] of the workers of iniquity.
Let the wicked fall into their own nets, whilst that I withal escape.

The apostle Paul wrote about his escape from a trap in 2 Corinthians 11:32-33:

> In Damascus the governor under Aretas the king kept the city of the Damascenes with a garrison, desirous to apprehend me:
> And through a window in a basket was I let down by the wall, and escaped his hands.

Paul's enemies had set a trap for him at the gates of the city, and "they watched the gates day and night to kill him" (Acts 9:24), but the disciples let him down by night over the wall in a basket. So Paul evaded his intended killers and got safely away from the danger.

In view of these facts there should be no doubt about our Lord's meaning when He told us to watch and pray that we may be worthy "to escape all these things that shall come to pass." Many translators support our view of *escape* in this text. We quote from two well-known translations (Other translators give similar meanings.).

> From hour to hour keep awake, praying that you may succeed in escaping all these dangers to come . . . (Moffatt)
> Beware of slumbering: at all times pray that you may be fully strengthened to escape from all these coming evils . . . (Weymouth)

Observe that it is from "all," not part of, these impending dangers, from all these imminent disasters, that we escape. And Jesus specified "that day" and the "snare" as "these things" that shall come to pass. And it is from these things that we are to pray to escape.

There are some texts that refer to *part* of the tribulation period, and other texts that refer to *all* of it. When Jesus used the term "that day," He included the entire judgmental period because He specified "all these things that shall come to pass." Some teachers argue that the Church must go through the first part of the tribulation, but this is in conflict with the meaning of the words that Jesus used.

Another point of proof is this: When Jesus told us to watch and pray "*that* ye may be accounted worthy to escape," the word "that" (*hina*) has reference to *purpose* and it means "in order that." [5]

So, when Jesus admonished us to watch and pray, it was for the purpose of—in order that—we shall escape all the dangers and disasters that begin with "that day."

We should also see the biblical meaning of the word "tribulation." The Greek word is *thlipsis*, and it signifies "pressing together, pressure, distress, afflictions . . . [it is used] of the distress of a woman in childbirth, Jn. 16:21." [6]

We now see the word tribulation for the birth-pangs of a pregnant woman in John 16:21:

> A woman when she is in travail hath sorrow, because her hour is come: but as soon as she is delivered of the child, she remembereth no more the anguish [tribulation].

Jesus used the same word when speaking of the tribulation judgments, "All these are the beginning of sorrows [birthpangs]" (Matt. 24:8). Paul used the same illustration in 1 Thessalonians 5:2-4:

> For yourselves know perfectly that the day of the Lord so cometh as a thief in the night.
> For when they shall say, Peace and safety; then sudden destruction cometh upon them, as travail upon a woman with child; and they shall not escape.

The entire period of the tribulation judgment is

illustrated by the birthpangs of a pregnant woman. The afflictions and anguish at the close of the age are the pains preceding the birth of the coming kingdom. Jesus referred to this new birth when He told about "the regeneration [new birth] when the Son of man shall sit in the throne of his glory" (Matt. 19:28).

The period of the judgments will be tribulation in the sense that it will be anguish, distress, and affliction, from beginning to end. The birthpains continue until the new kingdom is born when Christ returns.

CHAPTER 3

The Thief Illustration and the Escape

The thief illustration was a favorite with Jesus. He spoke three times about thieves and robbers in the parable of the Good Shepherd (John 10:1-14). The religious thief uses the sheep for his own selfish purpose and he steals and destroys their souls. "The thief cometh not but for to steal, and to kill, and to destroy."

The thief often conceals his character and seeks to avoid detection. He moves slowly and silently through the darkness and springs suddenly upon the unwary victim who thinks he is safe and secure. A thief is "one that comes without warning," and this is the chief characteristic stressed by Jesus and Paul and Peter in their admonitions about the need for vigilance to be ready for Christ's coming.

We now see how Jesus used this illustration as a warning to be ready for His coming. And observe that He used it in a context about the judgment that came upon the world in the time of Noah:

> But as the days of Noah were, so shall also the coming of the son of man be.
>
> For as in the days that were *before* the flood they

were eating and drinking, marrying and giving in marriage, until the day that Noah entered into the ark,

And knew not until the flood came, and took them all away; so shall also the coming of the Son of man be . . .

Watch therefore: for ye know not what hour your Lord doth come. But know this, that if the goodman of the house had known in what watch the thief would come, he would have watched, and would not have suffered his house to be broken up. (Matt. 24:37-43)

Jesus here spoke about what the people were doing before the Flood. They were living in excessive self-indulgence (surfeiting), and did not believe the warnings of Noah about the coming judgment. Noah was "a preacher of righteousness" (2 Pet. 2:5), but all his preaching fell on deaf ears. And as righteousness was the issue in the apostasy before the Flood, so also it is today. Jesus admonished us not to be over-charged (overpowered) with the indulgences and anxieties of this life.

As the world was living in unrighteousness before the Flood, so also shall it be at the time of Christ's coming. And so also shall it be before His coming, as revealed in Luke 17:26, "And as it was in the *days* of Noah, so shall it be in the *days* of the Son of man." Notice the use of the plural "days" because it is important. The tribulation period is here described as "the days of the Son of man." [1]

After telling about the flood judgment, Jesus added, "But know this, that if the goodman [house-holder] of the house had known in what watch the thief would come, he would have watched, and would not have suffered his house to be broken up" (Matt. 24:43).

Jesus used the words *but know this* to get their attention to what He was going to say about the thief—which was a truth they knew. If the householder had been alert, his house would not have been broken into. The thief comes only to steal, to kill, and to destroy. And the point of the thief story is that the owner could have prevented the loss and destruction.

Paul taught the thief lesson to the Thessalonians as we see in chapter 5:1-9 of the first epistle:

> But of the times and seasons, brethren, ye have no need that I write unto you.
> For yourselves know perfectly that the day of the Lord so cometh as a thief in the night.
> For when they shall say, Peace and safety; then sudden destruction cometh upon them, as travail upon a woman with child; and they shall not escape.
> But ye, brethren, are not in darkness, that *that day* should overtake you as a thief.
> Ye are all the children of light, and the children of the day: we are not of the night, nor of darkness.
> Therefore let us not sleep, as do others; but let us watch and be sober.
> For they that sleep sleep in the night: and they that be drunken are drunken in the night.
> But let us, who are of the day, be sober, putting on the breastplate of faith and love; and for an helmet, the hope of salvation. For God hath not appointed us to wrath, but to obtain salvation by our Lord Jesus Christ.

Paul told the Thessalonians it wasn't necessary for him to write to them about prophetic times and seasons because he had previously taught them that the day of the Lord cometh as a thief in the night. And from all the signs about the "day," Paul specified two—"peace and safety."

These times and seasons denote periods during

which prophetic events appear that could not happen at any other time. Each age has its own characteristics and opportunities. The Judas-mob had their time and opportunity: "This is your hour and the power of darkness."/So also today Satan has his season to set the world stage for the coming of Antichrist. Critical times are useful to Satan and he takes full advantage of them./

During these time periods there are successive stages of growth in prophetic signs, and there is a continual movement in the development of them until they reach final fulfillment. Consider the fast-developing Middle East sign, and the Israel sign: from a small beginning 25 years ago, to Israel's present powerful position, it has been described as "a miracle in the desert." The European Common Market and World Church signs are developing together with the other signs. Few signs have more importance or more details given to them than the world trade sign in Revelation 18. We get considerable information about this from daily news reports. It is necessary that these signs develop together with the peace-safety signs.

For many years world leaders have been promoting world peace. Catholic and Protestant world organizations have joined in the crusade. Thousands of ministers in America are working for it, and for a while it will be a reality.

The favorite theme of the Old Testament false prophets was "peace, peace," but it never came. It was their greatest delusion, and they deceived the people with it when war and slavery were imminent. They only prophesied things that were popular with the people, and they offered the people the promises of God without obedience to the commandments.

The true prophets told them the truth and were persecuted.

Peace and prosperity will be the most tempting bribe Satan has ever offered the nations. It will be the perfect bait, and desperate nations will go for it, "as a bird hasteth to the snare, and knoweth not that it is for his life" (Prov. 7:23).

From all the signs preceding the tribulation, Paul put the stress on two—peace and safety. It may be because these are the two most important. Some experts think that most of the world's problems are largely related to these two things.

It will be to a troubled world that Antichrist will flash his peace-prosperity lure. Antichrist will be a world sensation, and his supernatural solutions for the world's problems will be something the nations have never seen before.

Compare this with the fact that recent polls show that in America there is a "confidence crisis." More than two-thirds of the people have expressed no confidence in the heads of government, nor in the Congress, and worst of all, no confidence in the churches. Satan will have the world mind well prepared to accept Antichrist.

Some countries that are members of the United Nations have stated publicly that they have no confidence in its peace efforts. But they will say of Antichrist, "Who is like him?" "Who can make war with him?"

We do not know how long Antichrist will be here before the "day" begins, but it could be a considerable *season* while he is setting his trap. Daniel revealed that he will have a small beginning with a gradual rise to world domination. "He shall come up, and shall *become* strong with a small people"

(Dan. 11:23). Operating by the energies of a mysterious power, he will cast a hypnotic spell over the entire inhabited earth, and they will express their awe with two questions: Who is like the beast?—Who can make war with him? (Rev. 13:4). He will bring peace to the world because no nation—not even with nuclear weapons—will be able to make war with him. No military genius in history has been or can be his equal.

The world will be settled down in the ease and comfort of their peace-safety delusions when the sudden destruction strikes. (The idea of prosperity is included in the word "safety." Before it was used in the New Testament it had the meaning of "all is well.")

One of the first judgments of the "day" will be "to take peace from the earth" (Rev. 6:4), so the peace plan is in operation before the time of tribulation begins.

Paul said "*they* shall not escape" this sudden catastrophe. "*But ye*, brethren, are not in darkness, that *that day* should overtake you as a thief" (1 Thess. 5:4).

There is a distinct contrast here between "they" and "but ye." The English "but" has the identical meaning of the Greek and signifies "on the other hand." This means that two ideas are brought sharply into contrast by placing them side by side, and that the second idea should be compared and contrasted with the first.[2]

So, in the contrast of the two ideas, what Paul said was this: On the one hand, sudden destruction will come upon them and they shall not escape. On the other hand, the sudden destruction shall not come upon you, and you shall escape.

On the one hand, they are the sons of darkness; on the other hand, you are the sons of light. The destruction falls upon them because they are "of darkness." It does not fall upon you because you are "of light."

> The genitive *of darkness*, points to nature and origin. To *belong to* darkness is more than *to be in* darkness.[3] [Darkness is the element in which they exist.]

Another point of contrast is that the thief will "overtake" them but will not overtake you. This word (*katalambano*) signifies to take possession of by seizure—"to seize with hostile intent"—"to lay hold of so as to possess as one's own." [4] Jesus used this word in John 12:35-6:

> Walk while ye have the light, lest darkness come upon [*overtake*, RV] you: for he that walketh in darkness knoweth not whither he goeth.
> While ye have light, believe in the light, that ye may be the children of light.
> If therefore the light that is in thee be darkness, how great [intense] is that darkness! (Matt. 6:23)

Jesus, in Gethsemane, spoke of "the *power* of darkness." This is the enslaving and dominating spirit of darkness. And Paul mentioned the "rulers of the darkness of this world" (Eph. 6:12). These are ruling spirits that seize humans with hostile intent and bring them under their control. So Paul, in his contrast, said that in the seizure of that day, "they" would be overtaken, but not "ye."

This word is also found in the story of the boy seized by a demon spirit:

> And one of the multitude answered and said, Master, I have brought unto thee my son, which hath a dumb spirit;

> And wheresoever he taketh [*overtakes*] him, he
> teareth him: and he foameth, and gnasheth with
> his teeth, and pineth away. (Mark 9:17-18)

Can you imagine what it will be when these hordes of evil spirits are turned loose in "that day" to take possession of the world's masses who "loved darkness rather than light"? Darkness they loved, and darkness they shall get. As the plagues continue to come in the tribulation, Antichrist's "kingdom was full of darkness; and they gnawed their tongues for pain" (Rev. 16:10).

Paul made another contrast when he wrote about those who sleep and those who watch. "Therefore let us not sleep as do others; but let us watch and be sober. For they that sleep sleep in the night" (1 Thess. 5:6, 7). In this sleep-watch comparison, Paul said *they* sleep but *we* must watch and be sober. One of the Lord's judgments will be to cause *them* to "sleep a perpetual sleep, and not wake, saith the Lord" (Jer. 51:39). "They sink down ... into an eternal sleep of death." [5]

Paul also wrote about these perpetual sleepers, and said that "God hath given them the spirit of slumber." The result of this judgment follows in the verse: "eyes that they should not see, and ears that they should not hear" (Rom. 11:8).

We are sorry to say that after a long ministry, we have seen many of these sleepers in the churches. Nothing awakens them out of their indifference to the things of God, not even the truth about the coming of the Lord. Having willfully and persistently refused to awaken to spiritual things, they have been given over to their slumber.

Long indulgence in worldly pleasures has dulled

their spiritual senses until they are sunk in a moral stupor. They continue to sleep because darkness is the element in which they exist. May the terrors of "that day" awaken them.

We conclude that Jesus and Paul taught the same truth with the thief illustration. The Church will escape that day, the snare, and the sudden destruction of the world of peace and prosperity that men will have built.

CHAPTER 4

Salvation and the Escape

We shall quote again a part of the passage we saw in the last chapter and observe the word "salvation" that is used twice.

> But let us, who are of the day, be sober, putting on the breastplate of faith and love; and for an helmet, the hope of salvation.
>
> For God hath not appointed us to wrath, but to obtain salvation by our Lord Jesus Christ. (1 Thess. 5:8, 9)

We have seen that "escape" means "to get safely out of danger," and that "we" shall get safely out of the danger of the "sudden destruction," and that we shall get safely away from "that day"—the tribulation.

We see now that "salvation" here signifies that we shall be saved from the sudden destruction and the tribulation. Escape and salvation here have similar meanings. Both these words signify deliverance or safety from the judgments of "that day," or "the day of the Lord." In these verses (1 Thess. 5:2-4) we see another example of how these "day" terms interchange.

Paul again in I Thessalonians 5:8 said that we

are "of the day." In verse 5 he said that we are not of the night nor of darkness. We showed from the Greek text that this means *belonging* to the day, and *not belonging* to the tribulation night.[1]

Paul then illustrated his thought with the likeness of the armed soldier—the breastplate of faith and love, and the helmet of salvation. This is a symbol of victorious warfare. "For the weapons of our warfare are not carnal, but mighty through God to the pulling down of strong holds" (2 Cor. 10:4). They are also mighty through God in resisting the thief.

Paul's soldier is more than conqueror in the conflict. He is not seized and taken captive by the thief into the darkness. We saw that "overtake" means "to seize and take possession of with hostile intent." But Paul's symbolic soldier is *saved* in the battle because he is protected with the helmet of salvation.

The vigilant and armed soldier was one of Paul's favorite illustrations. He used it again in Ephesians 6:13-17:

> Wherefore take unto you the whole armour of God, that ye may be able to withstand in the evil day, and having done all, to stand.
> Stand therefore, having your loins girt about with truth, and having on the breastplate of righteousness;
> And your feet shod with the preparation of the gospel of peace;
> Above all, taking the shield of faith, wherewith ye shall be able to quench all the fiery darts of the wicked. And take the helmet of salvation, and the sword of the Spirit, which is the word of God.

The spiritual warrior will be victorious in "*the* evil day" because he is strong in the Lord and in the power of His might. The breastplate of righteousness, faith, love, and the helmet of salvation are his *protective* armor. He resists the enemy, and having done all—having conquered all—he leaves the field of battle in the victory of salvation.

As Paul twice used the word "salvation" in the sense of deliverance from the tribulation judgments it is important to establish the precise definition of this word.

Salvation (*soteria*) is a comprehensive or generic word, and it has wide meaning in Scripture as it also had among ancient Greeks. It means much more than the saving from sin.

> In the New Testament the word "salvation" . . . is sometimes applied to temporal benefits . . . to expound fully the contents of this term . . . would be to expound the contents of the Gospel.[2]

The words *save* and *salvation* appear about 150 times in the New Testament.

> Nearly a third of the New Testament references to salvation (and its verbal forms) denote, as so frequently in the Old Testament, deliverance from specific ills, such as captivity, disease, and devil possession.[3]

> Salvation (*soteria*) signifies to "bring out safely from a situation fraught with mortal danger." It is used, "of the evil days of the last tribulation."[4]

Other standard sources give similar meanings. Moulton and Milligan's *The Vocabulary of the Greek New Testament* is the highest authority of all:

> Salvation is common in the papyri in the general sense of "bodily health," "well-being," "safety."[5]

A few examples will illustrate these meanings.

Peter wrote that God "spared not the old world, but saved Noah, . . . a preacher of righteousness, bringing in the flood upon the world of the ungodly" (2 Pet. 2:5).

Genesis 19:16-22: In this account the word "escape" is used five times in connection with Lot's getting safely out of Sodom, and in verse 19 Lot spoke of the angel as "saving my life."

And as it was in the days of Noah and Lot, so also shall it be in the coming judgment. The sudden destruction shall come upon the ungodly but the righteous shall be saved.

Exodus 14:8-13: When it appeared that Pharaoh had Israel trapped at the Red Sea, and Israel was facing total destruction, Moses encouraged them, "Fear ye not, stand still, and see the salvation of the Lord" (v. 13). They escaped the trap by the miraculous passage through the sea.

Acts 27:20-44: During the voyage to Rome where Paul was to stand trial before Caesar, he warned the ship's captain that to continue the voyage would be with "hurt and much damage, not only of the lading and ship, but also of our lives" (v. 10).

They refused Paul's warning which proved true when they were caught in the tempestuous storm.

> And when neither sun nor stars in many days appeared, and no small tempest lay on us, and all hope that we should be *saved* was taken away. (v. 20)

When they were driven close to shore some of the shipmen were about to flee out of the ship, but Paul said to the centurion, "Except these abide in the ship, ye cannot be *saved*."

It was the soldiers' counsel to kill the prisoners, "lest any of them should swim out, and *escape* [flee away safely]" (v. 42). "But the centurion, willing to *save* Paul, kept them from their purpose" (v. 43).

All got safely to land by swimming or on boards

and broken pieces of the ship. "And so it came to pass, that they escaped all safe to land" (v. 44).

We conclude from these facts that when Paul twice used the word *salvation* in a passage about the tribulation judgments, he meant that we shall be delivered in safety out of these judgments.

We arrive at the same conclusion from his words in the passage, "For God hath *not appointed us to wrath*, but to obtain salvation by our Lord Jesus Christ" (1 Thess. 5:9). This wrath is the sudden destruction which "they shall not escape." They are appointed to it but we are appointed to salvation. The word "appoint" signifies "to put or place," and it was not God's purpose in choosing us to put us in this tribulation wrath. Other translations agree:

> For God has not destined us to the terrors of judgment. (The New English Bible)
>
> For God did not choose us to condemn us. (Phillips)
>
> For God has not destined us to incur His anger. (Weymouth)

CHAPTER 5

The World Temptation and the Escape

> Because thou hast kept the word of my patience,
> I also will keep thee from the hour of temptation
> which shall come upon all the world, to try them that
> dwell upon the earth. (Rev. 3:10)

This text is prophetic and Christ here speaks of
the final world trial preceding His coming that will
test the nations. He warned before about this world-
test in Luke 21:35, "For as a snare shall it come
on all them that dwell on the face of the whole earth."

The standard lexicons, revisions, and many
translations agree that this will be a special temptation (test) for the inhabited earth, and those who
keep the word of Christ will be kept safely from
it. We quote a few sources to show the meaning:

> Here it has the article, as if "*the* tempta-
> tion" were to be of no ordinary kind.

> "The hour of trial" seems to be that which
> Christ had foretold should precede his coming,
> especially the triumph of Antichrist. Hence the
> declaration in the next verse, "Behold I come
> quickly." [1]

> Rev. 3:10: "The great time of trouble which

shall be before the Lord's second coming. As such, it is immediately connected with *I come quickly*." [2]

Rev. 3:10: "The hour of [the] temptation —the appointed *season* of affliction (Deut. 4:34, the plagues are called 'the temptations of Egypt'): *the* sore temptation coming on: the great tribulation before Christ's second coming." [3]

In this text Christ promised believers that He would keep them in safety from the coming judgment, and that He would keep them from the time (hour) of the temptation.

It may be helpful to look at another passage which shows God's protection of Noah and Lot in times of judgment and see how the word "temptations" is used in the context.

For if God spared not the angels that sinned, but cast them down to hell, and delivered them into chains of darkness, to be reserved unto judgment;

And spared not the old world, but saved Noah a preacher of righteousness, bringing in the flood upon the world of the ungodly;

And turning the cities of Sodom and Gomorrha into ashes condemned them with an overthrow, making them an ensample unto those that after should live ungodly;

And delivered [rescued] just Lot, vexed with the filthy conversation of the wicked:

(For that righteous man dwelling among them, in seeing and hearing, vexed his righteous soul from day to day with their unlawful deeds;) The Lord knoweth how to deliver [rescue] the godly *out of* temptations [Gk. *trial*], and to reserve the unjust unto the day of judgment to be punished. (2 Pet. 2:4-9)

Here again we see a contrast between the godly

and ungodly in times of judgment when God put nations on trial. Noah and Lot were saved from the judgments that fell upon the ungodly who were condemned.

Noah was a preacher of righteousness, and the preflood world was put on trial by his message of righteousness. They rejected this and perished. But Noah was safely in the ark before a drop of the destructive waters fell. He was sealed against the judgment because "the Lord shut him in" (Gen. 7:16).

Likewise in Lot's case, no part of the fiery punishment fell upon him. The heavens were ready to burst with the impending disaster while the delivering angel hastened him to safety. The angel said, "I cannot do anything until thou be come thither," and Lot was forbidden to even stay in the plain, "lest thou be consumed" (Gen. 19:15-22). Lot did not live through any part of that judgment. He escaped "out of" it. It was a rescue from fiery judgment.

We cited above in Deuteronomy 4:34 that the demand for the freedom of the Israelites was a "temptation" to Pharaoh. This word is not always used in a bad sense but sometimes means to "test" or "prove." An example is in Genesis 22:1, "God did tempt Abraham."

Pharaoh hardened his heart under the trial, and the divine plagues afflicted his land. But in the punishments the Lord "put a difference between the Egyptians and Israel" (Ex. 11:7). The plagues of disease, pests, death and darkness did not come upon the Israelites in Goshen because the Lord told Pharaoh that He would "put a division between my people and thy people" (Ex. 8:20-24). The land of

Goshen was a sanctuary of protection for Israel during the temptation. And when there was thick darkness over Egypt, "even darkness that may be felt," all the "children of Israel had light in their dwellings" (Ex. 10:21-23). The Israelites were kept from that time of temptation and judgment.

After telling about the deliverances of Noah and Lot from the judgments in their times, Peter said, "The Lord knoweth how to deliver the godly out of temptations. . . ." And Jesus promised in Revelation 3:10, "I also will keep thee from the hour of temptation which shall come upon all the world." In both places, "out of" and "keep *from*," the same Greek *ek* (out of) is used and has the same meaning.

From these facts we think the meaning is evident that the Lord knows how to deliver, and that He will deliver the godly out of the worldwide temptation referred to in Revelation 3:10; and also in this text, Christ promised not only to keep the faithful out of this judgment but to keep them from the time of it.

Peter said the destructions in the times of Noah and Lot are "an ensample unto those that after should live ungodly." In these two cases, as in the Egyptian judgments, the Lord "put a difference" between the godly and the ungodly. Jesus and the apostles drew warnings from history. And in these verses we see historical illustrations of divine condemnation upon the ungodly and His protective care of the godly.

The word "ensample," or example, signifies "a copy, model, pattern, object-lesson." And in Peter's context it is an illustrative case to warn the ungodly—"those that *after* should live ungodly"—what they could expect in the future judgment. God condemned

Sodom and Gomorrha with an "overthrow" (Gk., *catastrophe*), and in the future catastrophe, according to the example, God will save and deliver the godly, as He saved and delivered Lot.

It was a complete salvation for Noah and Lot. They did not suffer any part of the catastrophes. Peter's use of the word *example* is against the thought of the sudden destruction striking the pre-tribulation Church. The "day" will bring salvation to the Church, not destruction.

We have seen the meaning of God's saving Noah and delivering Lot, and that the Lord knows how to deliver the godly out of temptation. So we return to Revelation 3:10 and apply what we have learned to Christ's promise to keep the faithful from "the hour of temptation which shall come upon all the world."

Our Lord's promise here reminds us that He taught us to pray, "And lead us not *into* temptation, but deliver [rescue] us from evil" (Matt. 6:13). And our question here is this: Can we pray that we shall not enter into this world trial? If not, why?

We cannot escape all temptation, but Jesus taught that we can avoid many temptations that Christians fall into, and we are to pray that we shall not "enter into" these. The Old Testament Hebrew scholar, R. B. Girdleston, wrote:

> When we ask God not to lead us into temptation, we mean, Lead us not into that position, and put us not into those circumstances in which we should be in danger of falling an easy pray to the assaults of Satan.[4]

Also, what did our Lord mean when He warned, "Watch and pray, that ye *enter not into* temptation"? (Matt. 26:41). We know that we cannot escape all temptations because the purpose of God for us is accomplished in them. This is taught in James 1:2-3:

> My brethren, count it all joy when ye fall into divers temptations;
> Knowing this, that the trying of your faith worketh patience.

But Christ clearly indicates it is His will that we do not enter into *the* temptation of Revelation 3:10. Why then cannot we pray that we shall not be led into this temptation? Why cannot we pray that we shall not *enter* into it? This temptation is another name for the snare of Luke 21:36. And as Jesus told us to pray to escape the snare, then we can *also* pray that we shall not enter into this temptation.

God put Israel to the proof by false prophets working signs and wonders. (See Deuteronomy 13:1-3.) These supernatural works were powerful temptations to lead Israel into idolatry. Antichrist will likewise deceive the nations with manifestations of supernatural power. Paul described this in 2 Thessalonians 2:9-12:

> Even him, whose coming is after the working of Satan with all power and signs and lying wonders,
> And with all deceivableness of unrighteousness in them that perish; because they received not the love of the truth, that they might be saved.
> And for this cause God shall send them strong delusion, that they should believe a lie:
> That they all might be damned who believed not the truth, but had pleasure in unrighteousness.

The miracle working power of Antichrist will amaze the world. His signs and wonders will be something the nations never saw before, and they will be powerful temptations for them to accept his claim to deity. We should note here that Antichrist sits in the temple, not as Christ, but as God, "shewing himself that he is God" (2 Thess. 2:4).

His lying wonders support his claim that he is God. This, with his peace-security solution for the world's troubles, is *the* lie. The *lying* wonders doesn't mean that the wonders are not real (as many think) because the same Greek words used for the signs and wonders of Christ are used for those of Antichrist. God allows this power to be "given" to him to deceive the nations (Rev. 13:1-5). "A *sign* is intended to appeal to the understanding, a *wonder* appeals to the imagination, a *power* indicates its source is supernatural." [5]

This worldwide temptation will be a snare, and the snare will be baited. There's an interesting point in James 1:14, "But every man is tempted, when he is drawn away [*baited*] of his own lust, and enticed." The nations will be baited with the peace-security lure. The satanic appeal will be to their lusts for material things, and a desperate and chaotic world will take the bait. All we have heard during the past few years about peace and security is only the beginning of a deceptive strategy to prepare the world mind for its acceptance.

This temptation is the forerunner of the tribulation (*thlipsis*), and this word has an interesting history. It signifies pressure, affliction, difficult circumstances, or extreme distress. In ancient England criminals were confined in cells so small that they could neither stand, sit, walk, nor lie in them at full length. Or they had "heavy weights placed on their breasts, and were so pressed and crushed to death, this was literally *tribulation*." [6]

The prophets saw the nations in distress and perplexity at the end time, and the pressure will increase until they are forced into the jaws of the baited trap.

Jesus was a disappointment to Jewish hopes. He was not the spectacular Messiah they expected. They desired a sensational deliverer to restore the kingdom to Israel but the Carpenter from Nazareth was a stumbling-block to their messianic dreams.

The Jews desired that Christ "would show them a sign from heaven" (Matt. 16:1). But He refused and replied that as sign-seekers they were "an evil and adulterous generation" (Matt. 12:39). They believed that only God could show supernatural signs from heaven, and they would believe on Christ if He would show them flashing rays of kingdom splendor from the heavens. But Jesus rejected requests for the spectacular as He did when He refused to cast himself down from the temple or to come down from the cross.

But Antichrist will fully satisfy the world's lust for the sensational. He will dazzle the eyes of an evil and adulterous generation with displays of the supernatural from heaven. Antichrist and his false prophet will perform mighty miracles, even making "fire come down from heaven on the earth in the sight of men" (Rev. 13:13). But Christ's promise is that He will keep the faithful out of Antichrist's miraculous temptations.

In Peter's verses we see a repetition of truths about Noah and Lot that we have seen previously. Jesus and the apostles did not avoid repetition. The same truths are stated again and again throughout the New Testament.

We also observe points of similarity between Luke 21:35-36 and Revelation 3:10.

In Luke, the world test is a "snare"; in Revelation, it is a "temptation."

In Luke, the world test comes on "all them that dwell on the face of the whole earth." In Revelation, it shall "come upon all the world, to try them that dwell upon the earth."

In Luke, we are told to pray to escape the snare. In Revelation, Christ promised to keep us from the hour of the temptation.

We conclude that the worldwide snare of Luke 21:35 and the worldwide temptation of Revelation 3:10 are the same event because there are not two such world events in the prophecies. And to escape the trap does not mean to be kept safe while caught in it.

CHAPTER 6

Signs That Precede the Tribulation

Things appear to be coming to a head practically everywhere in the world.[1]

Prophetic signs appear at certain times and seasons, and there is a time for the tribulation to begin. Jesus told about the beginning of sorrows and about events which "must first come to pass" (Matt. 24:8; Luke 21:9). Some signs will appear before the tribulation begins and others will appear after it begins. We are primarily interested in the first-signs or preliminary events which Jesus said would indicate that "the day" is near. Dates cannot be set, but we can know the nearness of "the day." We can "see the day *approaching*" (Heb. 10:25).

Jesus told the Pharisees about the weather signs which they could discern (Matt. 16:1-3). And as events can be predicted by observation in the natural sphere, so also events are discernible in the spiritual sphere. Thousands now save their lives by fleeing from hurricanes and tornados predicted by the weather man; and those who watch and pray will escape the tribulation. In both cases, the warnings provide escape from approaching danger.

Paul said there are "times and seasons" for these events (1 Thess. 5:1-3). *Times* refer to the duration of periods and *seasons* refer to shorter periods. Seasons are parts of times. In our time and season Satan has the opportunity to prepare the nations for Antichrist. The world stage must first be set for his appearance. We saw before that Jesus told the Judas-mob, "This is your hour and power of darkness."

There are successive periods to these prophetic seasons during which events happen that could not happen at any other time. And when one season ends, another opens, and the nations move from crisis to crisis with ever-increasing danger. In the Bible, the prophecies are represented as continually coming to pass until the ultimate realization is attained.

There will be preliminary events before the tribulation begins, as there are indications of springtime before it arrives. Jesus said we know when summer is near. And Jesus also said, "For as in the days *before* the flood . . . so shall also the coming of the Son of man be" (Matt. 24:38-39). Certain signs and conditions will appear first.

There will be sensational signs after the day of the Lord begins, but these will be after-signs. If there should be signs in the sun, moon, and stars before "the day" begins, then it would defeat the purpose of secrecy, and "the day" could not come "unawares," or as a thief in the night.

As there were preflood conditions before that judgment came, so also shall there be pretribulation conditions. It will be helpful and we will avoid confusion if we keep the first-signs and after-signs in their proper places. And this is not difficult to do if we observe indications of this in the texts and contexts of the prophecies.

Jesus spoke about first-signs in Luke 21:9, "But when ye shall hear of wars and commotions, be not terrified, for these things must first come to pass; but the end is not by and by [immediate]."

From this we learn that terrifying commotions will first be present in the world. This was true during the days before the Flood when "the earth also was corrupt before God, and the earth was filled with violence" (Gen. 6:11). "The wickedness of man was great in the earth"; they corrupted marriage and glutted themselves with eating, drinking, and sex until they were morally hopeless. They rejected Noah's message of righteousness and did not believe his warning about "things not seen as yet." Lawless, violent, and persistently wicked, they sank to the depths of apostasy and unbelief. The Spirit of the Lord withdrew His striving, and they were given up to their doom. All that God cannot redeem He will destroy.

As Jesus connected the word "terrified" with "commotions," it will be helpful to amplify the meaning of *commotions*. From leading Greek sources we gather these definitions: "Disorder, confusion, tumults, riots, upheavals, unruly, restless, uproar, anarchy, lawlessness, turbulence, conditions that terrorize, dreadful events that cause panic." The reader can judge whether these definitions describe what he sees in the world news reports.

As we are primarily interested in these first-signs, we shall note a few items of interest recently taken from news sources that deal with these commotions. Here's an item clipped from *U.S. News & World Report* March 12, 1973:

> In Brussels, a team of researchers is assembling data on "world problems." Definition: a problem

existing or recognized by three or more countries and documented by experts. Identified so far: 1,200. Total expected: Some 5,000.

These problems take many forms. In the United States from 1960 to 1969, crimes of violence rose ten times as fast as the population. Official figures show that during this period violent crimes rose from 285,200 in 1960 to 660,000 in 1969.

Another commotion in America is in family life. The U.S. Census Bureau reported that a few years ago there was one divorce for every seven marriages. But in 1971 there was one divorce for every three marriages. Another official report states there are about 1,000,000 teenage runaways each year.

The World Health Organization reports about the worldwide "suicide crisis," and says there are about 15,000 suicide attempts per day. Stress and depression are given as chief causes of suicide. One specialist wrote, "Every depressed person is a potential suicide." Two national magazines published a report about a high rate of suicide among psychiatrists. A specialist at Boston University School of Medicine, after observing 2,000 student patients, wrote: "The students I have seen are, in nearly 100 percent of the cases, in a state of depression."

A neurotic world is cracking under the stress of fear, disappointment, and pressure. One report on crime says that fear has become a part of life for millions of Americans, and that crime is spreading fast and is increasingly vicious. There were more that 600 riots in America in the five-year period between 1968 and 1973. With many other Americans listening to a television speech I heard the President say, "We live in an age of anarchy."

Jesus, in describing the terrifying pretribulation events, specified wars *and* commotions, with nation against nation. There have always been wars and commotions, but events preceding the day of the Lord will be worse. The prophecies stress the fact that the end-time world situation will be the most dangerous of all. Wars, commotions, and nation against nation all occurring together will be a frightful situation. Satan will frighten the world into accepting his peace-prosperity plan, and a frantic world will take it.

There has never been a world nuclear war, but military leaders envision the horrible possibility with hundreds of millions killed in the first attack. Scientists have repeatedly warned that mankind is sitting on the edge of disaster. The world's superpowers are engaged in a nuclear arms race, and the number of nations with nuclear weapons is increasing. The staggering cost of this arms race puts the nations under enormous financial pressure, and oppressive taxation follows.

The most crucial question confronting the United Nations today is this: "Can nuclear war be averted?"

The competitive superpowers are building huge war machines with thousands of nuclear bombs stockpiled. Russia and China are in continual conflict as they challenge each other for supremacy. The Soviet militarists have set their eyes on the industrial countries of Western Europe, and smaller nations are scared. The nations are choosing sides and forming alliances as seen in the North Atlantic Treaty Organization versus Russia's Warsaw Pact Nations. There will be other confederations in the Middle East, especially between northern and southern countries. The eleventh chapter of Daniel describes these al-

liances with one division headed by "the king of the
north," and the other division headed by "the king
of the south."

Military reports say that Russia continues to gain
in the Mideast. They continue to build up their powerful military forces there. The U.S. Sixth Fleet is also
there. Both sides are capable of massive destruction,
and the Mediterranean situation is described as "explosive." Satan will keep the nations in turmoil with
ever-increasing pressure.

Among the first-signs we also include the world's
economic crisis. Satan's end-time plan is peace *and*
prosperity. Most of the world's problems are related
to these two things, and Antichrist will work with
the old political slogan: "Give the people what they
want." Nations have various security plans because
their people are restless with a deep yearning for
security.

The prosperity of the European Common Market
has influenced other nations to apply for membership. Promoters of the Market believe that a unified
Europe is on the way and that a United States of
Europe will soon be a reality. Ten years ago the
eminent historian Arnold Toynbee said, "The time
for world government has come," and he was quoted
recently, "European unification will go on." Albert
Einstein said, "I also believe that world government
is certain to come in time."

The expanding European Market has enormous
power, and experts predict it may soon control 40
percent of world trade. It could then become a
dominant political and world power. It was a significant shift when Britain, in a changing world of power

balances, chose to join the Common Market. Nations once friendly to the United States now look to Europe for leadership. Existing alliances are being shaken and a new world is emerging.

The world-trade sign described in Revelation 18 appears on the horizon. This chapter is a graphic picture of "great riches" spread over the earth by international shipping. The major powers are in a race to build super cargo ships and tankers. Middle East countries own 80 percent of the free world's crude oil. As I write these lines, our Government is holding an emergency conference to deal with the energy crisis caused by the oil shortage. American shipyards that were closed a few years ago are being reopened and enlarged to build the superships. The supertransport era is here.

A new era with startling changes has come. For example, Japan rose from the ruins of war within one generation to become the dominant industrial power in Asia. Events with prophetic meaning are breaking fast on the world scene, and the nations realize they must chart a new course in world affairs. World trade has increased 339 percent since 1950, and maritime nations are in a race to dominate competitors in the world's markets. These and other facts indicate that a literal fulfillment of Revelation 18 is intended. The entire world is in a state of *change*, and this global change is necessary before the prophecies can be fulfilled. If anyone thinks that our thoughts about world changes are farfetched, let him read the nonreligious book, *Future Shock,* by Alvin Toffler, an expert in world affairs. Today's shocking changes are producing tomorrow's world.

No doubt about it, coming world transformations will stagger the nations—"like a drunkard" (Isa. 24:20).

The *uniworld* sign is also in the making. The one-world idea is not new but it is now moving closer to reality. The United Nations in its 1973 session almost accomplished its universal purpose to bring all nations into their membership. The United Nations now has 135 members, and with such a union, few nations desire to stay out. There are serious differences among members of the United Nations and changes may come, but the present universality appears to indicate a trend toward the end.

The *unichurch* sign is also developing with the uniworld sign. Both grow together and operate together until they become universal. In the end-time prophecies one does not appear without the other. About ten years ago I heard Bishop Sheen say it is the Roman Catholic purpose to bring all the world religions into one fold. And it was about the same time I heard a Protestant ecumenical leader say, "Most Protestants are now ready to accept the Pope as their spiritual leader." There has been an enlargement of all the signs since that time.

By unichurch we mean the *World Church*, which is that system of universal religion described in Revelation 17-18. A vast organizational merger of churches has been forming for years but the prophets saw a *union of spirit*, and they stressed this fact more than collective merger.

This world religious system is represented in the Bible under the symbol of a harlot. She represents the unfaithful or prostitute church. The prophets often used the words "harlot," "whoredom," "adultery," and "fornication" to describe her. In Revelation, chapters 17-18, her entire religious character is summed up in the word "fornication."

But the true and faithful Church is represented with the symbol of a bride, and her whole spiritual character is summed up in the word "righteousness" (Rev. 19:8). The difference between the Harlot Church and the Bride Church is the difference between fornication and righteousness.

The harlot is married to the world and world rulers and she "reigneth over the kings of the earth" (Rev. 17:18). Proud and boastful, she dominates kings and princes who have "lived deliciously with her." The "offence of the Cross" and the "reproach of Christ" have no part in her apostate theology. She has the inhabited earth intoxicated with the "wine of her fornication." She finds lovers in all nations, and she adapts herself to all classes and kinds. She is attractive and powerful and fascinates every tongue, tribe, and nation with her mystical charms. She has a golden cup in her hand "full of abominations and filthiness of her fornication" (Rev. 17:4), and this cup is filled with the *wine* of her fornication, which is "the *spirit* of whoredoms" (Hos. 4:12). All drink from this one cup because this is the universal spirit.

Many churches considered fundamental have not escaped the harlot's defiling spirit and teaching. They tolerate a spirit of worldly pleasures and have made concessions to the prevailing spirit of the times that is not conducive to spiritual fidelity. They have yielded to the pressures of popular opinion.

Even in apostolic times the churches were tempted with these dangers. Paul warned the Corinthians not to be seduced from "the simplicity that is in

Christ" (2 Cor. 11:3). He reminded them that Eve was deceived by the serpent's cunning and she was "beguiled," which means she was deceived with a *false reasoning.* The word "simplicity" signifies "single-hearted faithfulness," so Paul admonished them not to be led astray from single-hearted faithfulness to Christ by false reasoning. False doctrines are false reasonings, and this takes many forms in intellectual deception. It will reach its climax at the end time. The world has never seen the full force of Satan's deceptive power as it will be manifested in the Harlot Church. There is already much of it in the world.

In considering the first-signs that precede the escape of the Church before the tribulation begins, we should also point out the name-sign or number-sign of Antichrist which will be revealed to the true Church before Antichrist becomes a world power. The identity of Antichrist will be concealed in his name. This is described in Revelation 13:18:

> Here is wisdom. Let him that hath understanding count the number of the beast: for it is the number of a man; and his number is Six hundred threescore and six.

Antichrist will come as a savior to the world, and he will work in deep secrecy so as not to reveal his real character; his identity will be mysteriously hidden in his name. It will be more than a word puzzle or numerical riddle, and beyond the sphere of human intelligence to discern. To date all attempts to connect the number 666 with historical characters have failed.

As the harlot-woman has upon her forehead "a name written, MYSTERY" (Rev. 17:5-9), so also there is a mystery to the name of Antichrist. And as only "the mind which hath wisdom" can discern the harlot, so also only the wisdom and understanding given by the Holy Spirit will expose Antichrist.

Revelation 13:18 seems to suggest something like a satanic secret code. Dr. George Lamsa in his *The New Testament According to the Eastern Text*, which is a translation from the ancient Aramaic texts, used the words "code number" in this verse.

The end-time operations of Satan are summed up in the prophecies with two words—*deception* and *mystery*. And the latest world revival of the occult will be useful to Satan in his deceptive operations. There has never been a time when the Church needed the gifts of the Holy Spirit more than today, especially to detect the counterfeit working of Satan through extraordinary phenomena of the psychic mind. As the end approaches, God and Satan will fight the greatest battle of all, and it will be warfare in the realm of the supernatural.

The Israel sign is also developing together with the other signs. All lines of prophecy converge in Israel, and Jerusalem is the final center of all. Since the rebirth of the State of Israel, it has had a phenomenal growth. The prophecies for Israel deal with both the land and the people, and like other prophecies, they are being fulfilled as no other generation has seen them fulfilled. From a small beginning in 1948, Israel has become a power that withstands Russia and the Arab confederacy.

Israel, surviving crisis after crisis through the centuries, continues as one of God's wonders. This is due to the supernatural character of the covenants that God made with Abraham and David. Our Covenant-God has put himself under oath to these fathers, and every promise He made to them is a declaration of His will. His covenant name guarantees that every promise He made to them shall come to reality. One of God's favorite names for himself is "The God of Abraham." All biblical prophecy is related to these covenants, and all that God shall ever do in all eternity is related to them. There isn't a more significant sign of the times than the Israel sign.

The Mideast sign moves with the Israel sign. This comprises the countries of Daniel's image (Dan. 2). Arab nations are rising to positions of world power. All that we have seen and heard in world news reports about these countries are preliminary. Changes are coming fast in France, Portugal, Spain, West Germany, Italy, Yugoslavia, Romania, Greece, Turkey, Iraq, Iran, Egypt, Libya, Jordan, and Algeria. In this territory there will be the centers of the world common market, world trade, world church, and the rise and rule of Antichrist.

World events since World War II have been gathering momentum. Coercive systems are developing. Pressure tactics are used everywhere. The Arab oil embargo showed how other nations can be pressured into conformity to the will of a few nations.

Happening together with the other signs is the Joelic sign. Peter, on the day of Pentecost, quoted from the prophet Joel, "And it shall come to pass in the last days, saith God, I will pour out of my Spirit upon all flesh . . . " (Acts 2:17). This prophecy had a small fulfillment at Pentecost Day, but it is being accomplished today on a global scale as never seen before, and it will increase more and more as the end of the age approaches. The prophetic scope widens and the picture continues to enlarge.

The present worldwide outpouring of the Holy

Spirit is in preparation for the end-time harvest in all nations. Even in the worst part of the tribulation there will be the reaping of "a great multitude, which no man could number, of all nations, and kindreds, and people, and tongues . . . " In all church history there has never been such a world sweep of the Holy Spirit (Rev. 7:9-14).

Our Lord's command to His church is to take the gospel everywhere and to make disciples of all nations until the end of the age (Matt. 28:19-20). And He instructed us, "Pray ye therefore the Lord of the harvest, that he will send forth laborers into his harvest." As "the field is the world," His command is still in effect for us to pray that the Lord of the harvest will send laborers to the nations. "And this gospel of the kingdom shall be preached in all the world for a witness unto all nations; and *then* shall the end come" (Matt. 24:14).

What the "former rain" did for the beginning of the church age, the "latter rain" will do for the end of it. "Behold, the husbandman waiteth for the precious fruit of the earth, and hath long patience for it, until he receive the early and latter rain" (James 5:7). As the farmer works his fields with patience until the rains come, so also we work and pray in the Lord's harvest fields until He pours out the latter rain for another reaping.

Another reason for the worldwide Joelic diffusion of the Spirit is to impart prophetic knowledge among the nations. As John the Baptist was the forerunner of Christ to "prepare the way of the Lord," and as His disciples preceded Him to the towns and cities of Israel, so also the Holy Spirit is preparing His elect among the nations. To accomplish this requires a knowledge of the prophecies.

This profusion of knowledge was indicated when Joel wrote, "I will pour out of my spirit upon all flesh: and your sons and your daughters shall prophesy, and your young men shall see visions, and your old men shall dream dreams. And on my servants and on my handmaidens I will pour out in those days of my Spirit; and they shall prophesy." When Christ promised to send the Holy Spirit, He said, "And he will show you things to come." It is the work of the Holy Spirit to reveal prophetic truth and to show us future events. An angel told John that he was the fellowservant of John and of those "that have the testimony of Jesus ... for the testimony of Jesus is the spirit of prophecy" (Rev. 19:10). This means that those who have the anointed testimony of Jesus possess the spirit of prophetic inspiration. "For the truth revealed by Jesus is the inspiration of all prophecy" (Weymouth).

As God prepares to close the Gentile age, the Holy Spirit is moving with a special visitation to the Gentile nations, and the central truth of prophetic inspiration is that "the coming of the Lord draweth nigh."

We conclude from our brief look at the signs that there are important fulfillments on the world scene today. The Brussels team of experts some time ago said that they expected the list of world problems to go to 5,000. Wars and commotions are on the rise, but the peace movement continues to spread. Political candidates who campaign for peace and prosperity will be more apt to be elected.

The uniworld and unichurch signs show important gains, and likewise the world-trade sign; also, the Israel and Mideast signs. The Joelic sign looms larger among the nations than ever, and the expanding world-missionary effort is taking the gospel to the uttermost parts of the earth.

All parts of the prophetic picture will be prepared and ready to fit into the final and total plan.

CHAPTER 7

A Thousand Years As One Day

The apostle Peter wrote about scoffers who object to God's delay in fulfilling the prophecies. They can see no outward signs of Christ's coming, and in unbelief they say that all things have continued in the usual order from the beginning of creation. Peter quoted their unbelieving statement and answered them in his second epistle (3:3-9):

> Knowing this first, that there shall come in the last days scoffers, walking after their own lusts,
>
> And saying, Where is the promise of his coming? for since the fathers fell asleep, all things continue as they were from the beginning of the creation. . . .
>
> But, beloved, be not ignorant of this one thing, that one day is with the Lord as a thousand years, and a thousand years as one day.
>
> The Lord is not slack concerning his promise, as some men count slackness; but is longsuffering to us-ward, not willing that any should perish, but that all should come to repentance.
>
> But the day of the Lord will come as a thief in the night; in the which the heavens shall pass away with a great noise, and the elements shall melt with fervent heat, the earth also and the works that are therein shall be burned up . . .
>
> Nevertheless we, according to his promise, look

for new heavens and a new earth, wherein dwelleth righteousness.

To the scoffing complaint that God is slow in accomplishing His purpose, Peter replied that one day is with the Lord as a thousand years, and a thousand years as one day. God does not always need long periods of time to fulfill His prophetic word because He can do in one day what He has not done in a thousand years.

It isn't necessary for God to hurry nor tarry. He does not need to speed up nor slow down because He has appointed a time and season for every purpose under the sun. God's apparent delay does not mean that He is slack concerning His promises, but He is longsuffering to us, not willing that any should perish but that all should come to repentance.

The scoffers say that all things continue as they were from the beginning of creation, and this indicates they are looking for spectacular events that will signalize Christ's coming. But the signs of His coming are not such as they expect to see. If there should be alarming outward cosmic upheavals or sensational events such as they expect, then the Lord could not come unawares or as a thief in the night. The signs of "the day of the Lord" will not be recognized by the world but by the Church. The spirit of prophetic discernment is given only to the overcoming Church.

Peter answered the scoffers with the historical illustration of the flood judgment (vv. 5-6). "The long-suffering of God waited in the days of Noah, while the ark was a preparing" (1 Pet. 3:20). But when the judgment came, it came quickly. The sudden-ness of the destructive judgment was stressed by our Lord in Luke 17:26-29, "They did eat, they drank, they married wives, they were given in marriage, until the day [the very day] that Noah entered into the ark, and the flood came, and destroyed them all."

The same emphasis is given to the fiery judgment upon Sodom and Gomorrah. "Likewise also as it was in the days of Lot; they did eat, they drank, they bought, they sold, they planted, they builded; but the *same day* that Lot went out of Sodom it rained fire and brimstone from heaven, and destroyed them all." They were glutting themselves in their pleasures and indulgences up to the very hour when they were surprised with the startling swiftness of the sudden catastrophe. "Even thus shall it be in the day when the Son of man is revealed." Peter also wrote of those who "bring upon themselves swift destruction . . . whose judgment now of a long time lingereth not, and their damnation slumbereth not" (2 Pet. 2:1-3). Swift disaster is waiting for them and their impending doom will strike speedily, as in the days of Noah and Lot.

As the end approaches, God must accomplish much in a short time because of the large number of prophecies to be fulfilled. This prophetic project will be carried out and terminated by such a rapid succession of events that Jesus said it would all be done in the lifetime of the generation living at the time of final fulfillment. "Verily I say unto you, This generation shall not pass away, till all be fulfilled" (Luke 21:32). The severity and rapidity of the final judgments would destroy all flesh if God did not shorten the judgment period. "And except those days should be shortened, there should no flesh be saved" (Matt. 24:22).

Paul, writing about God's dealings with Jews and Gentiles, also told about the short work that God will do in the end time. "For he will finish the work, and cut it short in righteousness: because a short work will the Lord make upon the earth" (Rom. 9:22-30).

God will terminate His dealings with the nations without delay, and bring His purpose in the earth to a speedy completion. He is putting the nations and the churches to the test of righteousness. God puts the masses to the righteousness test and thus separates the remnants from the apostates and unbelievers.

A remnant is a spiritual minority or what is left remaining after a time of testing. In one sense a remnant can be a considerable number, but when compared with a nation or denomination it is small. Many are called but *few* are chosen. God selects the comparative few because they choose God's Word as the standard of righteousness and live accordingly, by faith in Christ. The *many* do not obtain this righteousness because they do not seek it through faith in Christ (Rom. 9:30-32).

Paul, apostle to the Gentiles, drew illustrations of remnants from Jewish history and used them as warnings to his Gentile churches. Israel's apostasies are held up to us by Paul as something to be avoided, and he said they are examples for us to take heed to. In all church history the apostasies produced the remnants. The reformations are interesting studies in remnants; and Paul said, "Even so then at this present time also there is a remnant according to the election of grace" (Rom. 11:5). So, as the end draws near, God will cut short and finish His purpose of gathering the remnants out of the nations.

Our time is a special season for God's visitation and preparation of the Gentiles into the kingdom of God. Paul wrote that "blindness in part is happened to Israel, until the fulness of the Gentiles be come in" (Rom. 11:25).

This word *fulness* signifies "full number," "full measure," "sum total," "that which makes something full or complete." [1] God is working among the Gentiles and pouring out His Spirit upon them to obtain this sum-total result. And it will continue until it includes "all nations, and kindreds, and people, and tongues" (Rev. 7:9-14). This agrees with our Lord's command that we take the gospel to all nations—unto the uttermost part of the earth—until the end of the age (Matt. 28:19-20; Acts 1:8).

We have seen that this global outpouring of the Spirit is a fulfillment of covenant prophecy. And the central point of the Abrahamic Covenant was that God would give Abraham a worldwide family of spiritual children. This is being done today as it has never been done before. No other generation could say as we can today about the fulfillment of covenant prophecy, "This is that" (Acts 2:16). This covenant purpose will accelerate until the end of the age.

When God destroys the dream world of peace and prosperity that apostate men will build, they will be overwhelmed at the speed with which the judgments come. In their lamentation over the sudden destruction of their fabulous empire they cry out again and again, "Alas, alas, that great city Babylon, that mighty city! for in *one hour* is thy judgment come . . . for in one hour so great riches is come to nought" (Rev. 18:10-17).

Peter's statement about a thousand years as one day reminds us of Psalm 90:4:

> For a thousand years in thy sight are but as yesterday when it is past, and as a watch in the night.

Considering the fast-moving tempo of world events today and the staggering changes out of which a new world is emerging as a setup for Antichrist, we should give all the more heed to our Lord's command in Mark 13:35-37:

> Watch ye therefore: for ye know not when the master of the house cometh, at even, or at midnight, or at the cockcrowing, or in the morning:
> Lest coming suddenly he find you sleeping.
> And what I say unto you I say unto all, Watch.

It is only by our loving obedience to this command that we shall be accounted worthy to escape all these things that shall come to pass.

CHAPTER 8

What It Means to Be Worthy to Escape

> Watch ye therefore, and pray always, that ye
> may be accounted worthy to escape all these things
> that shall come to pass, and to stand before the Son
> of man. (Luke 21:36)

Various versions have different translations of this
verse. Instead of "accounted worthy to escape,"
some have, "that ye may prevail to escape," or a
similar rendering. Greek authorities say that either
translation gives a good sense, and the *Amplified
New Testament* combines both thoughts in its translation:

> Keep awake then and watch at all times . . . pray-
> ing that you may have the full strength and ability
> and be accounted worthy to escape all these things
> [taken together] that will take place, and to stand
> in the presence of the Son of man [their bracket].

This word "worthy" is significant in the New Testament, and Jesus gave it considerable stress. The
Greek word is *axios*, and the standard lexicons give
it similar definitions. When used of persons, the word
has the meaning of "value" or "worth."

Axios, *worthy, fit.* "He is not worthy of me,—

does not deserve to belong to me," Mt. 10:37.[1]

Axios. The sense of *worth, value.* (Professor Deissmann is cited on this meaning from the inscriptions.[2])

Axios, of weight, worth, worthy, is said of persons and their deeds: (a) in a good sense, e.g., Matt. 10:10, 11, 13 (twice), 37 (twice), 38; 22:8 . . . [3]

We now look at a few of many references to see how this word is used in the New Testament.

John told the Jews who came to be baptized of him, "Bring forth therefore fruits meet [worthy, *axios*] for repentance" (Matt. 3:8).

John demands proof from these men of the new life before he administers baptism to them. The fruit is not the change of heart, but the acts which result from it.[4]

Jesus, John, and the apostles were united on the teaching that only those who bear the fruits of righteousness in their lives are genuine Christians, as the Greek text proves.[5]

We look now at the emphasis Jesus gave to "worthy":

And into whatsoever city or town ye shall enter, inquire who in it is worthy; and there abide till ye go thence . . .

And if the house be worthy, let your peace come upon it: but if it be not worthy, let your peace return to you.

He that loveth father or mother more than me is not worthy of me: and he that loveth son or daughter more than me is not worthy of me.

And he that taketh not his cross, and followeth after me, is not worthy of me. (Matt. 10:11, 13, 37, 38)

Jesus told about others who were not worthy because when they received an invitation to the marriage of the King's son, "they made light of it, and went their ways, one to his farm, another to his merchandise."

Then saith he to his servants, The wedding is ready, but they which were bidden were not worthy. (Matt. 22:5-8)

In Luke 10:7 we get another view, " . . . the laborer is worthy of his hire."

Paul continued this truth about worthiness in his epistles. "I . . . beseech you that ye walk worthy [live lives worthy] of the vocation wherewith ye are called" (Eph. 4:1).

That ye might walk worthy of the Lord unto all pleasing, being fruitful in every good work, and increasing in the knowledge of God. (Col. 1:10)

We are bound to thank God always for you . . . so that we ourselves glory in you in the churches of God for your patience and faith in all your persecutions and tribulations that ye endure: which is a manifest token of the righteous judgment of God, that ye may be counted worthy of the kingdom of God, for which ye also suffer. (2 Thess. 1:5)

Paul told the Thessalonians that God had a righteous purpose in proving them with the persecutions. For it was by their endurance in these afflictions that they showed themselves worthy of the kingdom of God. There was spiritual worth in their faith and patience, and these were fruits that God required for genuine repentance.

Paul did not mean they were earning their salvation by their endurance in the trials. To be worthy of the kingdom does not mean self-salvation. We reject any worthiness apart from the merits of Christ and believe that no sinner can save himself, no matter how many religious works he may do or how much he may suffer. If sinners could earn or merit salvation without Christ, then Christ died in vain.

But it is clear from Paul's epistles that he, like Christ, was absolute in his requirements for discipleship. He demanded a love for Christ that was above all other considerations and evidence of salvation was required.

To get the right view of Paul on salvation, we must look at *all* that he wrote on this subject. We shall fall into error if we pick and choose from his statements, as some do. Paul wrote about God's predestinating purpose in Ephesians 2:8-10:

> For by grace are ye saved through faith; and that not of yourselves: it is the gift of God:
> Not of works, lest any man should boast.
> For we are his workmanship, created in Christ Jesus unto good works, which God ordained that we should walk [live] in them.

There is a connecting link in the "good works" here with what Paul wrote about the patience, faith, and endurance of the Thessalonians. These good works are a life of righteous actions toward God and men, and by them we prove ourselves worthy of the kingdom. They are not the mere performance of religious duties that Paul described as the "works of the law" (Gal. 2:16). An example of this is the story Jesus told about the self-righteous Pharisee praying in the temple (Luke 18:9-14).

The works of the law and the works of faith are extreme opposites. The works of faith are "created in Christ Jesus," and are the results of God's workmanship in the heart and life. They are the effects produced by the Holy Spirit and are called "the fruit of the Spirit," as seen in Ephesians 5:8-10:

> For ye were sometimes darkness, but now are ye light in the Lord: walk as children of light:

> For the fruit of the Spirit is [consists] in all good-
> ness and righteousness and truth.
> Proving what is acceptable unto the Lord.

The sum of all that is acceptable to God is here summed up in three words: goodness, righteousness, truth. The word "proving" contains the idea of testing and trial. Those who continue to walk with God, in testing and trial, with the evidence of goodness, righteousness, and truth, are living proofs of what is acceptable to God. God proves that He might approve, and what is approved is accepted by Him. Those who do not qualify under His rules of proof are not accepted.

Trials are the means by which God proves faith, and it is proven faith that is "more precious than of gold that perisheth." And it is such faith that will be to the honor and glory of Christ and His saints at His appearing (1 Pet. 1:7).

Paul again wrote of the spiritual worth of the Thessalonians in relation to Christ's coming:

> Wherefore also we pray always for you, that our
> God would count you worthy of this calling, and
> fulfil all the good pleasure of his goodness, and the
> work of faith with power. (2 Thess. 1:11)

The Thessalonians were qualifying to be worthy by the test of Christ-created works. This "work of faith" was required, and through the proving God was fulfilling the good pleasure of His goodness. It is God's good pleasure to produce this spiritual fruit in human lives. They cannot do it without Christ. "The branch cannot bear fruit of itself" (John 15:4).

Throughout the New Testament there is a worth-worthless contrast that underlies all that Jesus and the apostles taught. Paul takes this truth all the way to the judgment seat, when, at Christ's coming, He will accept the worthy and reject the worthless. Paul wrote about this in 1 Corinthians 3:11-13:

> For other foundation can no man lay than that is laid, which is Jesus Christ.
>
> Now if any man build upon this foundation gold, silver, precious stones, wood, hay, stubble;
>
> Every man's work shall be made manifest: for *the day* shall declare [disclose] it, because it shall be revealed by fire; and the fire shall try every man's work of what sort it is.

In the Bible, gold, silver, and precious stones are used to typify valuable and nonflammable materials. But wood, hay, and stubble typify worthless and flammable materials. The apostolic thought of a spiritual house or temple runs through all the New Testament; and we see various expositions of this idea, especially in Ephesians and Hebrews. We also see representations of the selection and preparation of the valuable materials used to build the spiritual structure.

Paul, in the verses above, represents persons with no spiritual value as being worthless for use in the eternal spiritual temple. They do not possess the eternal qualities to pass the fiery test at the judgment seat, and they will be unfit for the kingdom purpose.

As every man's work shall be revealed in that day, Paul expressed concern for the final result of his labor. He told the Corinthians, "Are not ye my work in the Lord?" (1 Cor. 9:1). To be sure that all who were his "work" possessed the necessary qualities to survive the fire-test at Christ's coming, he urged the Corinthians to:

> Examine yourselves, whether ye be in the faith; prove your own selves. Know ye not your own selves, how that Jesus Christ is in you, except ye be reprobates [*counterfeits*]? (2 Cor. 13:5)

There are three big words here: examine, prove,

reprobates. "Examine" signifies to try or test, and "prove" relates to the result of the examination. "Examine [*trial*] implies a definite intent to ascertain their spiritual condition" (Vincent). "Examine, *try, make trial of, put to the test*, to discover what kind of a person someone is, 2 Cor. 13:5." [6]

The word "reprobate" had an interesting history even before it came into New Testament language. It was used to indicate what was counterfeit after the testing of money and metals. Job said, "When he hath tried me, I shall come forth as gold" (23:10). After God tested Israel, Jeremiah wrote, "Reprobate silver shall men call them, because the Lord hath rejected them" (6:30).

The testing determined what was counterfeit and what was genuine. And what was found to be counterfeit was disapproved or rejected as worthless. Paul required proof of genuine character from the Corinthians. An analysis of Paul's epistles shows him to have been always thinking about the fiery examination at the end. And he stressed again and again that the final result of every man's life and work can only be what the judgment seat will prove it to be.

There is much in popular Christendom today that is cheap and worthless. There is much spiritual devaluation by leaders and laity who reject "the whole counsel of God." Being tolerant and permissive of sin and worldliness, they have substituted tinkling brass for gold and silver. And they think it is negative to insist on the same demands for discipleship as did Jesus and Paul. It was to such a church that Christ sent this message:

> I counsel thee to buy of me gold tried in the fire, that thou mayest be rich; and white raiment, that

thou mayest be clothed, and that the shame of thy
nakedness do not appear; and anoint thine eyes with
eyesalve, that thou mayest see. (Rev. 3:18)

This Laodicean church was spiritually "poor"
(v. 17), and the Counselor advised them to buy His
proven gold of righteousness and spiritual purity.
He said they would be rich if they did.

But Paul said that salvation is "the gift of God."
Why then must we buy a free gift? Was Paul at
variance with Christ? Or was he at variance with
himself? After telling the Ephesians that salvation
is God's free gift, and not of works, he told the Phil-
ippians that he had "suffered the loss of all things
. . . that I may win Christ" (3:8).

By suffering the loss of highly valued things to
win Christ, Paul was obeying Christ who required
such loss from all who desired to follow Him. "He
that loseth his life for my sake shall find it." "He
that loveth his life shall lose it" (Matt. 10:39; John
12:25). No one can earn salvation with his works,
but we buy the things of God in the sense that we
must pay the price of self-denial and forsaking all
that He requires in order to serve Him.

The biblical writers gave one view of a subject
in one text. And we must gather these views and
bring them together. No method of interpretation
is a safe guide if it does not obey this rule. The
calamities of doctrinal history in the Christian church
were caused by interpreters who looked only at one
side of a subject.

The truth about spiritual worthiness that Paul
taught the Thessalonians was repeated to others, and
the repetition he gave to this indicates the importance
he attached to it. Paul, the inspired apostle, who
wrote to the Ephesians, "For by grace are ye saved

... it is the gift of God: not of works lest any man should boast," also wrote this to Titus:

> They profess that they know God; but in works they deny him, being abominable. and disobedient, and unto every good work reprobate. (1:16)

We have seen that *reprobate* relates to testing or proving, and here the test is that of good works. Paul wrote about those who professed to know God but their works were a denial and contradiction of their profession, "in their actions they disown him" (Weymouth).

Words and works must agree, but the works of these people proved them to be frauds and counterfeits and Paul said they were worthless to God's purpose. In the Bible God has given tests by which we can know who are true and false prophets, by which we can distinguish between truth and error, and by which we can recognize true and false believers. Whatever we are, our character will manifest itself in visible actions. Can you imagine what the result would be if we had no way to recognize the difference between truth and error?

Sometimes we are asked questions like these: "With so many different religions in the world, how can I know which is true?" (They all claim to be true.) "How can I know that I will be saved?" "How can I know that I was predestinated to salvation?"

How would you answer these questions? I don't know of a better answer than to quote 2 Peter 1:4-10:

> Whereby are given unto us exceeding great and precious promises: that by these ye might be partakers of the divine nature, having escaped the corruption that is in the world through lust.
> And beside this, giving all diligence, add to your

faith virtue [moral character]; and to virtue knowledge;

And to knowledge temperance; and to temperance patience; and to patience godliness;

And to godliness brotherly kindness; and to brotherly kindness charity [love].

For if these things be in you, and abound, they make you that ye shall neither be barren nor unfruitful in the knowledge of our Lord Jesus Christ.

But he that lacketh these things is blind, and cannot see afar off, and hath forgotten that he was purged from his old sins.

Wherefore the rather, brethren, give diligence to make your calling and election sure: for if ye do these things, ye shall never fall.

Peter here agrees with Jesus, John the Baptist, and Paul on the required fruits as evidence of a genuine profession of salvation. What they taught about moral fruits and being worthy of the kingdom is similar to what Peter said here: "Give diligence to make your calling and election sure: for if ye do these things, ye shall never fall."

In writing about our calling and election to salvation, Peter said we must be diligently adding moral character, knowledge, temperance, patience, godliness, brotherly kindness, and love. Three times he referred to "these things" as God's means of making our calling and election sure. God predestinated His elect people "to be conformed to the image of his Son" (Rom. 8:29), and *conformed* here signifies to be made into the moral and spiritual likeness of Christ. Peter said that those who lack these things that form the likeness of Christ are barren, unfruitful, blind, and cannot see afar off. They cannot see heavenly things, only the things of earth. God's calling and election is related to the doing of these things.

The fact is stressed in Peter's text that it is by the doing of these things that one puts his calling and election beyond all doubt, "If ye do these things, ye shall never fall." God has provided a means of certainty for salvation that leaves one in a state of assurance. Christ is the "surety" of our salvation (Heb. 7:22), and He said, "If ye continue in my word, then are ye my disciples indeed" (John 8:31). He confirms and guarantees His promise as we live and abide in His Word.

The Greek text supports our interpretation of Peter's words, "If ye do these things, ye shall never fall." A. T. Robertson, the renowned Greek scholar, wrote concerning these words: "*If ye do (poiountes)*. Present active circumstantial (conditional) participle of *poieo*, 'doing.' " [7]

This can be verified from other leading sources: "Doing these things—because these things are done. And the participle is conditional . . . " [8]

There are many other texts associated with this subject that teach the same truth. One example is James 1:12:

> Blessed is the man that endureth temptation [trial]: for when he is tried [approved], he shall receive the crown of life, which the Lord hath promised to them that love him.

We should note here that all God's provings are not for the purpose of exposing the counterfeit, but they are also used for the refining of the saints. The following quotation from Archbishop Trench explains this:

> The ore is not thrown into the refining pot—and this is the image which continually underlies the use of the word [*proving*] in the O.T., except in the expectation and belief that, whatever of dross

may be found mingled with it, yet it is not *all* dross, but that some good metal, and better now than before, will come forth from the fiery trial. It is ever so with the proofs to which He who sits as a Refiner in his Church submits his own; his intention in these being ever, not indeed to find his saints pure gold (for that He knows they are not), but to make them such; to purge out their dross, never to make evident that they are all dross.[9]

From these facts we conclude what Christ meant when He told us to watch and pray that we be accounted worthy to escape the tribulation judgments. Those are worthy who are "rich toward God," "rich in good works," "rich in faith," and possess spiritual wealth, "which is in the sight of God of great price" (Luke 12:21; 1 Tim. 6:18; James 2:5; 1 Pet. 3:4).

These are the people who shall be God's eternal treasure. They are His predestinated ones, elected to salvation, and "they shall never perish." The Lord's inheritance is His people.

CHAPTER 9

Fine Linen and the Bride of Christ

> Thou hast a few names even in Sardis which
> have not defiled their garments; and they shall
> walk with me in white; for they are worthy. (Rev.
> 3:4)

We now further consider the moral worthiness
of the saints, and we shall see this truth from another
angle. Those who have not "defiled their garments"
shall not only escape the day of the Lord but shall
be worthy to walk with Christ in white. But the opposite of this is also true: those who have defiled
their garments are unworthy and they shall not escape that day, nor shall they walk with Him in white.

The garment symbol is one of the most prominent
representations in the Bible. The wedding robe is
the Bridegroom's gift to His Bride, but she has to
put it on. It will be of much profit to us if we look
at this wedding symbol in detail and learn the deep
spiritual meaning that it represents.

From the prophets onward, God's relation to His
people is expressed in terms of marriage, and this
relation provides the most intimate basis of His dealings with the bridal church. Christ pictured the kingdom as a marriage feast—for which one must be

properly attired. He told about one guest who was not dressed in the wedding robe at the marriage of a king's son. When the king entered the wedding chamber in his palace for the ceremony, his searching eye spotted the unrobed guest. He was speechless when asked by the king how he could be so disrespectful of the marriage custom, "Friend, how camest thou in hither not having a wedding garment?" The king was angered by the affront, for which there was no excuse, and commanded the servants to bind him and to cast him into outer darkness (Matt. 22:11-13).

Paul gave symbolic expression to the undefiled character of the Bride when he said the Church will be presented "as a chaste virgin to Christ" (2 Cor. 11:2). Undefiled by other lovers, and her virgin character preserved, she is admired by all heaven on her wedding day as a marvel of holiness. Standing beside her eternal Lover for the wedding ceremony, she is a miracle of righteousness. All heaven is interested in the beauty of her wedding robe and how she had prepared herself for the marriage. Angels and archangels gaze in wonder at the bridal scene in Revelation 19:6-9:

> And I heard as it were the voice of a great multitude, and as the voice of many waters, and as the voice of mighty thunderings, saying, Alleluia: for the Lord omnipotent reigneth.
>
> Let us be glad and rejoice, and give honor to him: for the marriage of the Lamb is come, and his wife hath made herself ready.
>
> And to her was granted that she should be arrayed in fine linen, clean and white: for the fine linen is the righteousness of saints.
>
> And he saith unto me, Write, Blessed are they which are called unto the marriage supper of the

Lamb. And he saith unto me, These are the true
sayings of God.

The New Testament purpose was revealed before
the birth of John the Baptist who was to go before
the Lord and "make ready a people prepared for
the Lord" (Luke 1:17). This was the keynote, the
main idea, the guiding principle, the central truth
of all New Testament teaching and preaching. This
was the message of John, Jesus, and the apostles.
An analysis of all that Jesus taught about His coming
shows that preparation for it was the point most
emphasized. He condensed an entire discourse about
His coming into two words—*be ready*. A people,
ready and prepared—this is the heart and center
of it all.

In two other places in Revelation Jesus used the
garment symbol to represent godly character:

> I counsel thee to buy of me gold tried in the fire,
> that thou mayest be rich; and white raiment, that
> thou mayest be clothed, and that the shame of thy
> nakedness do not appear; and anoint thine eyes
> with eyesalve, that thou mayest see.
>
> Behold, I come as a thief. Blessed is he that
> watcheth, and keepeth his garments, lest he walk
> naked, and they see his shame. (3:18; 16:15)

The virgin character of the Bride Church is represented by fine linen, "for the fine linen is the righteousness of saints." And what we want to know
here is the meaning of "the righteousness of saints."
It was "granted" to them to be attired in the linen
robe. They had obeyed His invitation to "buy of me
white raiment that thou mayest be clothed," so it
isn't self-righteousness; yet the language of the text
precisely states that it was the righteousness of the
saints. So, what does it mean?

The authoritative Arndt & Gingrich says, "The basic text for the New Testament is Eberhard Nestle's edition, 1952." [1] In the *Literal English Translation* (Alfred Marshall, translator) of this basic text, we read in Revelation 19:8:

> And to her was granted that she should be arrayed in fine linen, clean and white; for the fine linen is the righteous *deeds* of the saints.

This translation is supported by Thayer, Abbot-Smith, Cremer, Vincent, Vine, Hastings, Robertson, *The Amplified New Testament*, and many others. Henry Alford's comment on this verse is interesting.

> The righteousness of the saints, i.e., their pure and holy state.... Observe that here and everywhere, the white robe is not Christ's righteousness imputed or put on, but *the saint's righteousness,* by virtue of being washed in His blood. It is *their own*; inherent, not imputed; but their own by their part in and union to Him. [2]

Alford makes a sharp distinction here, but he was careful to say that the saint's righteousness is "by virtue of being washed in His blood," etc.

Paul said the bridal union between Christ and the Church is "a great mystery" (Eph. 5:32), and the divine enigma by which two become one is left unexplained. In the miraculous fusion, our will is united in oneness of spirit with His will, and our love is wedded to His love. Christ is our life, and that which constitutes His divine existence becomes the substance of our existence. In the creation of His eternal purpose within us His divine energy continually exerts itself. This life manifests itself by bringing us into conformity to what He is and all that He requires, and this results in righteous deeds and actions. Without such deeds and actions one is not righteous. The apostle John explained it like this:

> If ye know that he [Christ] is righteous, ye know that every one that *doeth* righteousness is born of him.
>
> Little children, let no man deceive you: he that *doeth* righteousness is righteous, even as he is righteous. . . .
>
> In this the children of God are manifest, and the children of the devil: whosoever *doeth not* righteousness is not of God, neither he that loveth not his brother. (1 John 2:29; 3:7, 10)

As righteousness is the test by which we distinguish children of God from children of the devil, and as this life of righteous deeds and actions is represented by fine linen, we now take a closer look into the subject of fine linen.

From all the fabrics in the world, why did the Lord select fine linen to represent His Bride? Why not silk or some other fiber? Linen is the better symbol because it more aptly illustrates the spiritual *preparation* necessary to be worthy to escape the day of the Lord and to walk with Christ.

Linen was made from flax, and there are about ninety kinds of flax plants. They are small herbs or shrubs with various colored leaves and flowers, and the plants usually grow from one to four feet high. They grow best in rich soil and in a cool, moist climate. In the ancient method of processing, from eighteen months to two years were required from harvesting to marketing.

Fine linen was the clothing of kings and queens. Their coronation robes were made with it. It was used in the hangings of the tabernacle, and the high priest was attired with it on the Day of Atonement. Vestments worn for special occasions were made with it, and it was the clothing of the wealthy.

When honors were bestowed upon persons, they were given robes of fine linen to wear at the ceremonies honoring them. Wedding robes for both bride and bridegroom were made with it. The Levitical choirs were robed in fine linen, and with it "garments of glory and beauty" were made for the Aaronic priests. The white-robed throngs in Revelation are dressed in linen. It was an expensive fabric of high quality, and as an article of merchandise it ranked with gold, silver, and precious gems.

In the ancient method of preparing the flax for the weaver, the stalks were soaked in water and then put through a process called *breaking*. This crushed the stalk to separate the fibers from the course, woody bark. Tools called "beaters" with flat wooden blades were used to hit and scrape the crushed stalks.

After the soaking, beating, and crushing, a further process of *separation* was called *combing* because a comb-like tool was used to remove other coarse parts. This combing was repeated again and again. A thorough preparation was necessary to produce *fine* linen. The finished product that came from the loom would only be as good as the preparation made for it.

The spiritual truth drawn from this emphasizes our separation or consecration to the Lord, which is a major Bible doctrine much neglected today in the churches. And this willful neglect has caused the Holy Spirit to depart from many of them. Paul applied this truth to the Corinthian church: "Wherefore come out from among them, and be ye separate, saith the Lord, and touch not the unclean thing; and I will receive you" (2 Cor. 6:17).

There is a vivid description of the World Church—

the harlot church Babylon—in Revelation 18:4, where God commands: "Come out of her, my people, that ye be not partakers of her sins, and that ye receive not of her plagues." This is God's warning to multitudes today. And many are obeying His command for separation as the Holy Spirit in His worldwide operation is preparing the Bride for her Bridegroom. This separation is the righteousness of the saints.

After combing, the flax was put through repeated washings. If the washings were not thorough, spots and blemishes would show up later and mar the quality of the linen. It was not allowed to go to the next process until all impurity had been washed out.

At each point of our spiritual preparation we must yield to the Holy Spirit's efforts to create in us the righteousness of Christ. A defective preparation of the flax produced a defective result. Old carnal habits and the former self-life continually reappear if there is not a thorough cleansing of the soul.

James wrote, "Let patience have her perfect work, that ye may be perfect and entire, wanting nothing" (1:4). The word *perfect* here signifies *complete*. We are to obey the Lord as He works out His will in our lives unto the completed end.

Paul had this final completion in view when he wrote that Christ died for the Church, "that he might sanctify and cleanse it with the washing of water by the word, that he might present it to himself a glorious church, not having spot, or wrinkle, or any such thing; but that it should be holy and without blemish" (Eph. 5:26-27).

Jesus told Peter, "If I wash thee not, thou hast no part with me" (John 13:8). We can have no part with Christ, no part in the Bride, and no part in His kingdom without this "washing of the water by the word." This sanctification or holiness is another forgotten truth in the churches, but the Lord will revive it again as He prepares the Bride for His coming. This washing and cleansing produces "the righteousness of saints."

The next process was sun-bleaching. The washed flax was exposed to the sun for curing and bleaching. The sun's fiery heat and penetrating rays gave it the bright luster and snowy whiteness emphasized in Scripture. Sun-bleached linens were best because artificial bleaching oxidized and destroyed the natural gum—and thus weakened the fibers.

Flax was one of the strongest and most durable natural fibers known, and it had many industrial uses. But if not properly processed, flax was weak.

We see much spiritual weakness in churches today. Jesus taught that some believers are weak and temporary (Matt. 13:21). But when we move in the divine progression, we "go from strength to strength" and are made "strong in the Lord, and in the power of his might."

Fine linen also had special quality as a preservative. Egyptian mummies 4,000 years old have been found wrapped in linen. Jesus was buried in linen clothes. We read that the Dead Sea Scrolls were found wrapped in linen. Paul prayed that our "whole spirit and soul and body be preserved blameless unto the coming of our Lord Jesus Christ" (1 Thess. 5:23).

Pure linen was not only clean and white but unmixed with other fibers. God gave Israel a law against such mixture, "Thou shalt not wear a garment of divers sorts, as of woolen and linen together" (Deut. 22:11).

In all church history Satan has succeeded in enticing many into a mixed religious life. The history of reformations and revivals is a record of conflicts with these mixtures to keep the gospel pure. Those who will not accept the pure gospel will take a mixture—a mingling of truth and error, the carnal and spiritual, the pure and impure, the righteous and unrighteous, the Christ-life and the self-life, the natural mind and the spiritual mind.

Paul admonished the Corinthians against such mixture when he wrote, "Ye cannot drink the cup of the Lord and the cup of devils." Those who tried to mix these two would "provoke the Lord to jealousy" (1 Cor. 10:21-22).

In our permissive age, many churches allow such a mixture of God and the world; but God will not accept a divided worship. The Harlot Church has a special blend that is deceiving multitudes everywhere. Paul wrote about harlot-church leaders in his day when he said, "For we are not as many which corrupt [adulterate] the word of God" (2 Cor. 2:17). These teachers were playing up the attractive positive part of the Gospel but watering down what they felt was the unattractive, negative part. They preached that God was love, but did not preach that He would be a God of vengeance to all who rejected His love. They were afraid to "declare the *whole* counsel of God."

Some textile manufacturers tried to deceive buyers by mixing adulterants with fine linen. Cotton was a chief adulterant, and this cheapened and weakened the fabric. But buyers used infallible tests to detect adulteration. Two such tests were to boil a sample of the fabric in water, or to set the fabric in the sun. Either test exposed the inferior material.

Jesus said, "Blessed are the pure in heart; for they shall see God." And the apostles wrote of pure minds, pure conscience, and pure religion. The biblical sense of spiritual purity is not only that we must be cleansed from sin but also that in our hearts there must be no polluting mixture. Some have a mingling of two minds, and to them James wrote, "Purify your hearts, ye doubleminded" (4:8).

The final work with the flax was spinning and weaving. The care in preparing it was evident in the finished product, but much depended on the skill of the weaver. Proper threading of the loom was important; also it was necessary to keep the threads at the right tension so as not to get a loose weave, and for this proper weights were attached to the loom. Density and texture were necessary to the quality of the linen, and the weaver used beaters to accomplish this.

The workmanship of the weaver was so evident in the finished product that buyers in the textile markets could sometimes recognize from which country the linen came.

In God's textile mill the specifications for fine linen are exact and the standards high. No detail is ever compromised. The workmanship of the divine Weaver is evident in His products. Satan imitates and counterfeits but he cannot duplicate the righteousness of Christ in His saints. All other world religions cannot compare with this.

After final inspection and approval, the linen was sent to the textile markets. Jesus taught that there will be a final inspection of all who enter the kingdom of God (Matt. 25:21). The apostle James wrote, "Blessed is the man that endureth temptation: for when he is tried [approved], he shall receive the crown of life" (1:12). "Well done, thou good and faithful servant . . . enter thou into the joy of thy

Lord." The servant had *proved* that he was both good and faithful. The purpose of testings and provings is to determine who shall be approved and who shall be disapproved. This is one of the most frequent and most emphasized truths in the New Testament.[3] There is a masterly exposition of this point in Trench's *Synonyms of the New Testament* (pp. 278-81).

It is often of deep interest to me to observe that biblical truths, spread over a wide area of Scripture, are sometimes summed up in one or two simple words. Example: All the qualifications for Christ's Bride are expressed in one comprehensive word—*righteousness*. It was given to the Bride to be attired in fine linen, but she "*made herself* ready." "Who will be in the Bride?" Those who have proved themselves righteous.

The wedding robe is the Bridegroom's gift to the Bride, but she has to put it on. Paul used the illustration of dressing and undressing when he wrote: "Put off . . . the old man . . . and put on the new man, which after God is created in righteousness and true holiness" (Eph. 4:22-24). "Put ye on the Lord Jesus Christ" (Rom. 13:14).

Those who obey the Bridegroom's command to be ready when He comes will share the privilege of reigning with Him forever in His "kingdom wherein dwelleth righteousness."

In view of all that this truth teaches about our preparation for Christ's coming, why is it so much neglected in the churches today? I heard recently about a minister who told his people, "You don't have to do anything to be ready for the coming of the Lord." Many will not see that they have been deceived until it is too late.

On a recently nationally televised program, the best-known Roman Catholic dignitary in America was asked this question, "What is the most pressing problem in the Roman Catholic Church today?" I was surprised when the Archbishop answered with one word: "Holiness!" It is also the most pressing problem in the Protestant churches.

When Christ said there were a few [limited number] in Sardis worthy to walk with Him in white, all thought of self-merit for salvation is excluded, yet the Bridegroom recognized the holy character of the few because they had not defiled their garments. Christ appreciates their love, faith, and worship. The spiritual worth of the Bride has eternal value to the Bridegroom.

CHAPTER 10

Replies to Objections

Those who have fully studied this subject about the Church and the tribulation will know that many leading Bible expositors teach that the Church must pass through the entire length of the tribulation period. Others teach that it will only pass through part of it, and both sides have submitted various arguments in their books to sustain their positions. We shall reply to what we think are the strongest of their arguments.

Objection 1. "The early church fathers of the first four centuries did not believe in a pretribulation Rapture. Nor did the great Reformation preachers, nor did the outstanding church leaders—Luther, Calvin, Edwards, Wesley, and many others. Can YOU prove a pretribulation Rapture?"

We reply that we respect the church fathers and the reformation leaders, but they are not the final authorities on a Bible doctrine. They did not agree among themselves on many important doctrines.

It is not necessary to our position to prove a pretribulation Rapture. Our Lord told us to pray that we shall "escape all these things." And this "escape" is the same word used by Paul on the same subject. It has not been our purpose to prove a pretribulation Rapture but pretribulation escape. So, the issue is not *rapture* but *escape*. We shall hold to the words that Jesus and the apostles used and not substitute other words in their places.

Objection 2. "From Acts 2:34-5, it is clear that Christ will remain at the Father's right hand until Armageddon; therefore, the Rapture cannot take place until after Armageddon which is after the great tribulation (1 Thess. 4:16-17)."

These texts in no way conflict with our view of pretribulation escape. Other texts state a similar fact about Christ, as in Acts 3:20-21, "Whom the heavens must receive until the restitution of all things . . . ," but these texts prove nothing against the overcoming Church escaping the snare of the day of the Lord.

Objection 3. "At His second coming, Christ will come with clouds (Matt. 24:30). This will be the visible appearing of Christ after the great tribulation. And this is the coming with clouds when we shall be caught up 'in the clouds' to meet the Lord in the air (1 Thess. 4:17). Therefore, the Church must endure the entire tribulation period."

This objection is similar to the last two. There is nothing in the references in this objection to refute the facts contained in the definition of "escape" that we quoted from leading lexical sources.

Our objectors seem to think there can be no escape of pretribulation believers until the Second Coming of Christ. Some quote Matthew 24:13-14, "But he that shall endure unto the end, the same shall be saved." But they fail to distinguish between those who are overcomers *before* the day of the Lord begins, and those who are overcomers *after* it begins.

"Escape" means "to get safely out of danger," and as pretribulation overcomers get safely out of the tribulation danger, how do they endure it unto the end? *Escape* and *endure* are two very different words, and "escape all these things" does not mean to "endure" them to the end of the judgment period.

Another point to notice here is that those who endure unto the end of the judgment period are *saved*—"the same shall be saved." Their salvation will be after endurance unto the end. But we saw in 1 Thessalonians 5:9 that the salvation of the pretribulation believers is at the beginning of the day of wrath, "For God hath not appointed us to wrath, but to obtain salvation by our Lord Jesus Christ."

Objection 4. "Christians have suffered persecution and tribulation through 19 centuries of church history. Why then should they be exempt from the tribulation of the day of the Lord?"

All Christians did not suffer persecution and tribulation in church history. Some had remarkable deliverances. This was also true in Old Testament times. Some were burned to death, others "quenched the violence of fire." Some were "slain with the sword," others "escaped the edge of the sword." The apostles James and Peter were imprisoned. James was killed with the sword, but Peter was saved from the sword by an angel (Heb. 11:32-37; Acts 12:1-10). Why? Nobody can explain this because it is one of the mysteries of God's will.

When Jesus wept over Jerusalem, He uttered a prophecy that saved the lives of the Christians in the destruction of the city in A.D. 70.

> And when he was come near, he beheld the city, and wept over it, Saying, If thou hadst known, even thou, at least in this thy day, the things which belong unto thy peace! but now they are hid from thine eyes.

> For the days shall come upon thee, that thine ene-
> mies shall cast a trench about thee, and compass
> thee round, and keep thee in on every side,
>
> And shall lay thee even with the ground, and thy
> children within thee; and they shall not leave in
> thee one stone upon another; because thou knewest
> not the time of thy visitation. (Luke 19:41-44)

Christ here predicted the strategy of the Roman
General Titus when he besieged the city before its
destruction in A.D. 70. He encircled the city with
trenches and the inhabitants were surrounded and
shut in on every side. But the Christians fled during
the early part of the long siege and escaped safely
to Pella in northern Peraea.

Dr. Alfred Edersheim, the New Testament Jewish authority, wrote about this escape in his *The
Life and Times of Jesus the Messiah.* He said there
were two dangers for the Christians at the time.

> Its twofold dangers would be—outwardly, the
> difficulties and perils which at that time would
> necessarily beset men, and especially the members
> of the infant church; and, religiously, the pretensions
> and claims of false Christs or prophets at a period
> when all Jewish thinking and expectancy would lead
> men to anticipate the near Advent of the Messiah.
> [A false prophet appeared during the siege and
> predicted Messiah would come and bring them de-
> liverance.—GD] There can be no question, that
> from both these dangers the warning of the Lord
> delivered the Church. As directed by him, the mem-
> bers of the Christian Church fled at an early period
> of the siege of Jerusalem to Pella, while the words
> in which He had told that His Coming would not be
> in secret, but with the brightness of that lightning
> which shot across the sky, prevented not only their
> being deceived, but perhaps even the record, if
> not the rise of many who otherwise would have
> deceived them.[1]

Dr. Edersheim also cites the historians Eusebius

and Josephus in support of his statement about the escape of the Christians.

So *Eusebius* (Hist. Eccl. iii. 5) relates that the Christians of Judaea fled to Pella, on the northern boundary of Peraea, in 68 A.D. Comp also Jos. [Josephus]. Wars iv. 9.1, v. 10.1.[2]

Dr. Philip Schaff, one of the most respected church historians, wrote about the destruction of Jerusalem in A.D. 70—"the most soul-stirring struggle of all ancient history." More than one million Jews in the crowded city were slain and many thousands perished from starvation. Another 97,000 were carried captive and sold into slavery. The Jewish rebels, in starvation and hopeless desperation, became "crazy fanatics" who murdered their own wives, children, mothers and fathers, slashing the throats of all who talked about surrender.

"Clinging with a last convulsive grasp to their Messianic hopes, [they] rested in the declaration of a false prophet, that God in the midst of the conflagration of the Temple would give a signal for the deliverance of His people." It was a cruel deception and the fearful judgment and prediction of Jesus was carried out to the uttermost. But the Christians had heeded the Lord's warning and escaped in safety to Pella.

The Christians of Jerusalem, remembering the Lord's admonition, forsook the doomed city in good time and fled to the town of Pella in the Decapolis, beyond the Jordan in the north of Perea, where King Herod Agrippa II., before whom Paul once stood, opened to them a safe asylum.[3]

The *purpose* of Christ in giving the signs about the destruction was that the Christians might escape the horrible calamity that befell the others.

And it appears to me that the signs and warnings that Christ gave about the end-time tribulation are fuller and more specific than the sign He gave about the destruction of Jerusalem. And the purpose of these signs and warnings is that we might escape the calamity. This fact has not been refuted by the ablest authors on the other side of this question.

Dr. A. T. Robertson was known in the world of Greek scholarship as "the foremost Greek scholar of modern times," and he wrote concerning the meaning of the words in Luke 21:36:

> Watch ye therefore, and pray always, that ye may be accounted worthy to escape all these things that shall come to pass . . .
>
> *But watch ye . . .* keep awake and be ready is the pith of Christ's warning. *That ye may prevail to escape . . .* First aorist active subjunctive with *hina* of purpose. The verb *katischuo* means to have strength against (cf. Matt. 16:18) . . . *Ekphugein* is second aorist active infinitive, to escape out.[4]

Objection 5. "Christians will not escape the tribulation period. They will escape the wrath of God but not the wrath of man. And as they will not escape the wrath of man they must endure unto the end."

In the Olivet Discourse, Jesus taught that the entire period of apocalyptic judgment would be a time of wrath—both the wrath of God and the wrath of man. This time period extends from the "beginning of sorrows" until the "end" of the sorrows. The Greek word for *sorrow* here, and *travail* in 1 Thessalonians 5:3, is *odin*, or "birthpang." Jesus and Paul both used the illustration of the birthpangs of the pregnant woman. Jesus said the entire period of the judgments would be sorrows, or birthpangs. When Jesus told us to pray to escape all these things, He meant the entire period of wrath, both of God and man.

Multitudes of believers will be killed by the wrath of man during the time of sorrows. John saw the souls of those that had been martyred during the first part of the sorrows. "I saw under the altar the souls of them that were slain for the word of God, and for the testimony which they held . . . and it was said unto them that they should rest yet for a little season, until their fellowservants also and their brethren, that should be killed as they were, should be fulfilled" (Rev. 6:9-11). And in Revelation 13:7, it is stated concerning Antichrist, "And it was given unto him to make war with the saints and to overcome them: and power was given him over all kindreds, and tongues, and nations."

War against the saints.

But there are some from the kindreds and nations who escape all or part of the judgments—after the judgments begin.

During the first part of the sorrows John wrote about the sealing of the 144,000:

> And I saw another angel ascending from the east, having the seal of the living God: and he cried with a loud voice to the four angels to whom it was given to hurt the earth and the sea.
> Saying, Hurt not the earth, neither the sea, nor the trees, till we have sealed the servants of our God in their foreheads. And I heard the number of them which were sealed: and there were sealed an hundred and forty and four thousand of all the tribes of the children of Israel. (Rev. 7:2-4)

This number are "sealed" from the impending calamity. They do not endure it. They are called "the servants of God," and we know nothing more about them until they appear with Christ on Mount Sion (Rev. 14:1). All the guesswork and speculation about what they do as servants of God is useless.

But the point we notice here is that they are sealed against both the wrath of God and the wrath of Antichrist. They escape with "the seal of the living God." So, we cannot see why it should be unreasonable to believe that others shall escape "the day" *before* it begins, especially since our Lord admonished us to watch and pray for the purpose of escaping it.

In Revelation 12:13-17, we read of others who will escape the tribulation wrath. Here the tribulation Church is represented by the woman symbol:

> And when the dragon saw that he was cast unto the earth, he persecuted the woman which brought forth the manchild.
>
> And to the woman were given two wings of a great eagle that she might fly into the wilderness, into her place, where she is nourished for a time, and times, and half a time, from the face of the serpent.
>
> And the serpent cast out of his mouth water as a flood after the woman, that he might cause her to be carried away of the flood. And the earth helped the woman, and the earth opened her mouth, and swallowed up the flood which the dragon cast out of his mouth.
>
> And the dragon was wroth with the woman, and went to make war with the remnant of her seed, which keep the commandments of God, and have the testimony of Jesus Christ.

The tribulation Church, like the Church today, will be those "which keep the commandments of God, and have the testimony of Jesus Christ." During the worst part of the tribulation Satan will be cast down to earth, "having great wrath, because he knoweth that he hath but a short time" (v. 12). He then turns against the Church with torrents of great wrath in an effort to destroy it. But "the earth helped the woman" and she escaped to a place of protection and nourishment "where she hath a place prepared of God" (v. 6).

Frustrated by the earth's help to the woman, and unable to penetrate her place of safety, the enraged Adversary goes to make war with the remnant of the woman's seed (the rest of her children).

There are other groups in the New Testament prophecies who escape both the wrath of God and the wrath of Satan and man during the tribulation judgments, but the two cases we have described should be sufficient.

Objection 6. "Paul placed the rapture of the Church at the time of the 'last trump; for the trumpet shall sound, and the dead shall be raised . . .' (1 Cor. 15:52). Paul also wrote in 1 Thessalonians 4:16-17:

> For the Lord himself shall descend from heaven with a shout, with the voice of the archangel, and with the trump of God: and the dead in Christ shall rise first.
>
> *Then* we which are alive and remain shall be caught up together with them in the clouds, to meet the Lord in the air.

"So, as the time of the rapture is at the *coming* of the Lord, which is the Second Coming, and the Second Coming is after the last trump, a pretribulation Rapture is impossible."

It is not our purpose to enter into the complicated debate about a pretribulation Rapture. The burden of our thesis is to prove a pretribulation escape for those who satisfy the conditions of Luke 21:36: "Watch and pray always, that ye may be accounted worthy to escape all these things that shall come to pass [*the things about to happen*]."

There is nothing in our escape texts that is inconsistent with the rapture texts quoted by our opponents. But the meaning they argue from their texts is inconsistent with the meaning of our texts. They violate an important rule of interpretation which says, "An interpretation must not only be consistent with one text; it must not be inconsistent with other texts." What we claim for *escape* is in no way inconsistent with what they claim for the time of the Rapture.

Objection 7. "When Jesus taught about the separation of the wheat and tares at the end of the age, He said:

> Let both grow together until the harvest: and in the time of harvest I will say to the reapers, Gather ye together *first* the tares, and bind them in bundles to burn them: but gather the wheat into my barn . . .
> As therefore the tares are gathered and burned in the fire; so shall it be in the end of this world. (Matt. 13:30-40)"

Again, we reply to this objection as to the previous one. Our view of the escape texts is not in conflict with the facts of the texts quoted in this objection. Also, we previously showed there are groups of believers who escape the tribulation judgments before the end when the tares are gathered to be burned and the wheat is gathered into the barn.

Objection 8. It is denied by opponents that the tribulation or day of the Lord begins "when they shall say, Peace and safety; then sudden destruction cometh upon them, as travail upon a woman with child; and they shall not escape" (1 Thess. 5:2-3). It is argued that the day of the Lord begins at the Second Coming of Christ, and the battle of Armageddon will be the "sudden destruction."

But if this be true, when shall there be the time of peace and safety? The tribulation is the "beginning of sorrows," and after the beginning there are increasing sorrows all the way to the end. The tribulation is a "day of wrath," and the divine wrath increases in intensity unto "the great tribulation." And His anger is so severe all the way to the end that "except those days be shortened, there should no flesh be saved" (Matt. 24:21-22). When shall there be the period of peace and safety if not before the beginning of the sorrows?

Paul said the sudden destruction cometh upon "them" as a thief and they shall not escape. But "ye" are not seized (overtaken) by the thief and shall escape.

The beginning of the sorrows and judgments is described in Revelation 6:1-4, and we read in verse 4:

> And there went out another horse that was red: and power was *given* to him that sat thereon to take peace from the earth, and that they should kill one another: and there was *given* unto him a great sword.

It is twice stated here that power and a great sword were given to the red-horse rider "to take peace from the earth." The word "given" indicates that the source of power given to the rider to take away the peace was supernatural.

It is argued by some that the peace here is not actual but only a wish or desire for peace because it will be "when they shall *say*, Peace and safety." Paul did not write when there shall *be* peace and safety. The form of Paul's statement indicates that peace and safety will not be the actual condition of the world but only a wish or expectation of men.[5]

With the rapid succession of the judgments, and the increasing intensity of them to the end, there is no time for the period of peace and safety after the plagues begin. It will be a time of God's anger, not a time of peace.

Also, it seems unreasonable to us that God would give the red-horse rider supernatural power to take peace from the earth if it were not an actual condition of the world. Would God send sudden destruction upon a mere wish or expectation of peace?

Paul wrote about the *coming* of Antichrist in 2 Thessalonians 2:7-11:

> For the mystery of iniquity doth already work: only he who now letteth [hinders] will let, until he be taken out of the way.
>
> And then shall that Wicked be revealed, whom the Lord shall consume with the spirit of his mouth, and shall destroy with the brightness of his coming:
>
> Even him, whose coming is after the working of Satan with all power and signs and lying wonders,
>
> And with all deceivableness of unrighteousness in them that perish; because they received not the love of the truth, that they might be saved.
>
> And for this cause God shall send them strong delusion, that they should believe a lie:
>
> That they all might be damned who believed not the truth, but had pleasure in unrighteousness.

Paul said the mystery of lawlessness was already operating in his day. And the spirit of it has been accumulating through the centuries, and it will continue until it produces Antichrist who will be the embodiment of all that the mystery is. The antichrist sign is now larger than ever.

The Apostle John also wrote about the appearance of the antichrist spirit:

> Little children, it is the last time; and as ye have heard that anti-christ shall come, even now are there many anti-christs; whereby we know it is the last time. (1 John 2:18)

When John observed the antichrist-sign nineteen centuries ago he connected the sign with prophetic time—"whereby we know it is the last time." And in our day this sign is developing into its final stage. John said that he who denies that Jesus is the Christ is both a liar and an anti-christ (v. 22).

There are millions more antichrists in the world today than ever. They are everywhere, even in large segments of Christendom, biblical seminaries, and popular churches. Some of the larger denominations are swarming with antichrists. This is a part of the total mystery which is having a gradual manifestation in our day.

Satan adapts himself to times and conditions, and he will have the world scene ready for the appearance of his Antichrist who will have a gradual rise to world domination.

Paul said that Antichrist's coming would be with all the strength of Satan's energy—"with all power and signs of lying wonders and with all deceivableness of unrighteousness." Paul could hardly have given a more inclusive description of the supernatural character of Antichrist than when he said that this mystery man will deceive the world with all kinds of miracles, signs, and marvels. The nations will be in desperate need of supernatural solutions to their problems, but instead of turning to Christ, they will turn to Antichrist.

The inhabited earth will be hypnotized with this satanic superman. They follow him in amazement, saying, "Who is like unto the beast? Who can make war with him?" (Rev. 13:4). The people worship him because of his superior military might. No nation will be able to make war with him—not even nuclear nations. And as no one can make war with him, then only he can enforce peace. He will satisfy the world's need for peace and prosperity.

A war-weary world yearns for peace. While I write these pages (January, 1974), there comes a national news report that our secretary of state, in a national poll, has been voted "The most admired man in America." This is because of his peace efforts in the Vietnam war and his peace-trade negotiations with Communist Russia and China. It is easy to believe that a hopeless world, perplexed in its dilemmas, will gladly take Satan's peace-prosperity bait and his coming superman.

It is further objected that the day of the Lord will come at the time of the battle of Armageddon, not at the beginning of the tribulation judgments. And this view is defended with the argument that "the day of the Lord so cometh as a thief in the night" (1 Thess. 5:1-2).

> But of the times and seasons, brethren, ye have no need that I write unto you.
> For yourselves know perfectly that the day of the Lord so cometh as a thief in the night.

This argument says that the thief-in-the-night illustration appears in post-tribulation contexts in Matthew 24:37-44; and in Revelation 16:15. So, it will be at the Second Coming that Christ will come as a thief in the night. Let's check this argument with a few facts to see if it is true or false, and we must remember that the important idea of the thief metaphor is "surprise—secrecy—without warning—unawares."

In the Olivet Discourse Christ told about frightful events that would be warnings of His approaching second coming. He said there would be . . .

> . . . fearful sights and great signs shall there be

from heaven . . . And there shall be signs in the sun, and in the moon, and in the stars; and upon the earth distress of nations [not peace and safety], with perplexity; the sea and the waves roaring;

Men's hearts failing them for fear, and for *looking after* those things which are coming on the earth: for the powers of heaven shall be shaken.

And then shall they see the Son of man coming in a cloud with power and great glory. (Luke 21:11, 25-28)

In Revelation 6:13-17, preceding the Second Coming, we read:

And the stars of heaven fell unto the earth . . . and the heaven departed as a scroll . . . and the kings of the earth, and the great men . . . and every bondman, and every free man, hid themselves in the dens and in the rocks of the mountains;

And said to the mountains and rocks, Fall on us, and hide us from the face of him that sitteth on the throne, and from the wrath of the Lamb:

For the great day of his wrath is come; and who shall be able to stand?

Also in Revelation 14:6-10, "Every nation, and kindred, and tongue, and people" will know that the Second Coming is near when the angel flying in midheaven warns them not to accept the mark of the beast.

When the heavens are shaken during the judgments and Satan is cast down to the earth, he will have "great wrath, because he knoweth that he hath but a short time" until the Second Coming (Rev. 12:12).

How will Satan know that he has only a "short time" until the Second Coming? How will he know when to gather his world armies at Armageddon to oppose Christ at His coming? He will not know the day nor the hour but he will know when it is near.

It isn't necessary to enter into a full explanation of the subject here, but there are specified periods of days, months, and times (Dan. 7:25; 12:5-12; Rev. 11:2; 13:5). From these periods the time of the Second Coming can be closely figured, but not the day nor the hour. Also, Satan can know from the various prophetic fulfillments and heavenly signs when he has a short time left.

How then could the Second Coming or the day of the Lord come as a thief in surprise and secrecy when Satan and his mobilized world armies are waiting and ready to enter into battle with Christ? (The battle will be fought at Jerusalem, not at Armageddon which is the place of mobilization. All who have been there know what an ideal situation it is for Satan's purpose.)

No such signs or time periods like those above are given to warn about the beginning of sorrows. This is when the day of the Lord will come without warning, in surprise and secrecy—"as a snare." The peace-and-safety sign that Paul gave the Thessalonians is a sign that the world will not recognize. And when a pleasure-loving and materialistic world is making merry with their false peace and prosperity, God's lightning flash of destruction strikes their dream world, "and *they* shall not escape. But *ye*, brethren, are not in darkness, that that day should overtake you as a thief." (Note that "the day of the Lord" and "that day" have the same meaning here in the context of 1 Thess. 5:1-4.)

From these and other considerations we conclude that the beginning of sorrows is the starting point of the day of the Lord, and that it is from this starting point that the above time periods in Daniel and Revelation can be figured—and in the same way,

Satan and others will know when there is but a short time to the end. They will not be surprised when Christ appears.

There is a long and sad history to date setting for the return of Christ. Even honorable names in biblical scholarship have devised ingenious chronologies for the time of Christ's coming, but time proved them wrong. They went wrong because they did not have the right starting point. They could have avoided their errors if they had taken heed to the signs that Jesus and Paul gave us.

Objection 9. "When Jesus told about the days of Noah and Lot, He made a distinction between 'days' (plural) and the 'day' (singular) 'when the Son of man shall be revealed.' "

The point of this objection is that the eating and drinking, buying and selling, marrying and giving in marriage, will be a world condition immediately preceding His coming, and not a pretribulation condition. We look now at the reference in Luke 17:26-30:

> And as it was in the *days* of Noah, so shall it be also in the *days* of the Son of man.
>
> They did eat, they drank, they married wives, they were given in marriage, until the day that Noah entered into the ark, and the flood came, and destroyed them all.
>
> Likewise also as it was in the days of Lot; they did eat, they drank, they bought, they sold, they planted, they builded;
>
> But the same day that Lot went out of Sodom it rained fire and brimstone from heaven, and destroyed them all.
>
> Even thus shall it be in the *day* when the Son of man is revealed.

Considering the varied uses of *days* and *day*, we do not think the distinction between the plural and singular is sufficient here to conclusively settle the question at issue, not even when both appear in the same context. We must consider other facts in the context and other passages bearing on the question. This we shall do and let the reader be the judge.

Our reply to this objection is similar to our reply to the last objection. After the beginning of the tribulation judgments the woeful plagues come in rapid succession and there will be no long periods of relief for the world to enjoy the lusts of life and the peace-prosperity boom described by Jesus. In Revelation 11:7-14, during a time of "woe," the people make merry because Antichrist will kill the two prophets who had previously "tormented them." But their rejoicing is short-lived because after three and a half days the prophets are resurrected and the thunderous judgments come crashing upon their heads again. Long periods of time would be required for the events described by Jesus in the above texts.

We should give careful study to the Noah-Lot comparisons that Jesus made with our day. *As* it was in the days of Noah, *so* shall it be *also* in the days of the Son of man. *As it was* in the days of Lot ... *even thus* shall it be in the day when the Son of man is revealed. ["Exactly so will it be" (Weymouth).]

We now *look* at Matthew's record of the Noah comparison.

> For as in the days that were *before* the flood they were eating and drinking, marrying and giving in marriage, until the day that Noah entered into the ark,
> And *knew not* until the flood came, and took them all away; so shall also the coming of the Son of man be. (Matt. 24:37-38)

Jesus seems to stress the point that the people

were glutting themselves in their indulgences up "until the day that Noah entered into the ark." His warning was about what they were doing *before* the flood, not *after* it. Noah was safely in the ark and *then* the flood came (Luke 17:26-27).

"Likewise as it was in the days of Lot." The warning is about what they were doing before the fire and brimstone fell. "But the *same day* that Lot went out of Sodom it rained fire and brimstone." Lot was safely out of Sodom and *then* the fire fell. Noah and Lot were in their places of safety before any part of the judgments fell.

Jesus added a significant detail to the comparison between Lot's days and ours when He admonished:

> Remember Lot's wife.
> Whosoever shall seek to save his life shall lose it; and whosoever shall lose his life shall preserve it. (Luke 17:32-33)

What was it about this woman that Jesus wants us to remember? She was not involved in the sodomitical sins. She was not a mocker about the impending destruction like her sons-in-law. She held the hand of the delivering angel as she was escaping the doomed city, and she got part way to the place of safety. Then, she was lost while she was being saved. And the sin and unbelief of her heart that brought God's punishment upon her is expressed in two words: she "looked back" (Gen. 19).

In remembering her, did Jesus mean that if we don't look back, the coming judgment will not fall on us as condemnation fell upon her? Did He mean that she *would* have escaped with her husband *before* any part of the fiery condemnation fell upon Sodom if she had not looked back?

In Lot's day, as in Noah's, the people made gods

of their possessions and pleasures. Jesus gave as much emphasis to this as to their sins of illicit marriage and remarriage. To them, as with multitudes today, these things are "life." "Whosoever shall seek to save his life shall lose it." Jesus taught much about life, and when Lot's wife looked back, it was with an intense yearning for those things that were life to her. Jesus called it "stuff in the house" (v. 31). Lot's wife lost both her stuff and her life. She looked backward to Sodom, but Lot's heart was in Zoar.

Lot's wife typifies many who merely believe what the prophecies teach about the coming tribulation but will not escape it. She represents a multitude of professing Christians who are not living in obedience to our Lord's warning: "But take heed to yourselves, lest your souls be weighed down with self-indulgence and drunkenness or the anxieties of this life, and that day come upon you, suddenly, like a falling trap; for it will come on all the dwellers on the face of the whole earth" (Luke 21:35, Weymouth). The anxieties of life are here put together with the excesses of eating and drinking (v. 34).

After telling us to remember Lot's wife, Jesus said, "Whosoever shall lose his life shall *preserve* it." And this word "preserve" means "to save alive." It includes both spiritual and physical salvation.

From the above considerations the evidence is decisive for the view that when our Lord used the Noah-Lot-Lot's-wife *examples*, He was speaking about total deliverance from the tribulation punishments. By all fair rules of interpretation, He conveyed the thought of complete escape before the catastrophic events of the tribulation begin.

Some prominent expositors believe that Isaiah

26:20-21 is a prophecy about the escape of the Church from tribulation wrath. And they use the Noah-Lot escapes as illustrations of this. We shall first quote this prophecy with comments on it by the Hebrew commentators Keil & Delitzsch in their *Old Testament Commentaries*.

Come, my people, enter thou into thy chambers, and shut thy doors about thee: hide thyself as it were for a little moment, until the indignation be overpast.

For, behold, the Lord cometh out of his place to punish the inhabitants of the earth for their iniquity . . .

It is thoroughly characteristic of Isaiah, that the commencement of this prophecy, like chapter 19:1, places us at once in the very midst of the catastrophe, and condenses the contents of the subsequent picture of judgment into a few rapid, vigorous, vivid, and comprehensive clauses . . .

(The) standpoint of prophecy is incessantly oscillating backwards and forwards in these four chapters (24-27). 'Go in, my people, into thy chambers, and shut the door behind thee; hide thyself a little moment, till the judgment of wrath passes by. For, behold, Jehovah goeth out from His place to visit the iniquity of the inhabitants of the earth upon them.'

The judgment only lasts a little while . . . a short time which is shortened for the elect's sake (not Israel's only).

Just as Noah, behind whom Jehovah shut the door of the ark, was hidden in the ark while the water-floods of the judgment poured down without, so should the church be shut off from the world without in its life of prayer, because a judgment of Jehovah was at hand.

We see the following in the Jamieson, Fausset and Brown *Commentary on the Whole Bible*:

"Come, my people, enter into thy chambers." When God is about to take vengeance on the ungodly, the saints will be shut in by Him in a place of safety, as Noah and his family were in the days of the flood (Gen. 7:16), and as Israel was commanded not to go out of doors on the night of the slaying of the Egyptian firstborn (Exodus 12:22-23; "The Lord will pass over the door, and will not suffer the destroyer to come into your houses to smite you") Ps. 31:20; 83:3 ("Thy hidden ones").

The saints are calmly and confidently to await the issue (Exodus 14:13-14). There was a Zoar for Lot in the destruction of Sodom, and a Pella for Christians in the destruction of Jerusalem by the Romans.

We saw previously that 2 Peter 2:4-9 contains the same truth about Noah and Lot. Leading New Testament scholars agree that verses 4 to 9 are a *unit of thought* because Peter's thought begins in verse 4 and follows through to verse 9. So, after telling about the "examples" of Noah and Lot, Peter closed his thought in verse 9 with the words, "The Lord knoweth how to deliver the godly out of temptations"—as He delivered Noah and Lot. *How* they will be delivered Peter left unexplained.

We also saw that the word for *temptations* here is the same word in Revelation 3:10, "Because thou hast kept the word of my patience, I also will keep thee from the hour of temptation, which shall come upon all the world, to try [test] them that dwell upon the earth."

The Lord knoweth *how*. We can rest and be satisfied with that. He knew how to make Goshen a haven of safety for the Israelites during the Egyptian plagues. He knew how to deliver Noah and Lot with the ark and angels, and how to provide a sanctuary of protection for the escape of the Christians from the destruction of Jerusalem in A.D. 70. He will know how to deliver the 144,000 with the seal of the living God, and He will know how to have "a place prepared of God" for the fleeing Church during the time of the tribulation persecution. And He will know how to deliver us.

Our Lord admonished us to "watch and pray, lest ye *enter into* temptation." With these facts before us, the will of God is clearly discerned. In loving obedience, we kneel before Him, and pray:

> Our Father which art in heaven . . .
> Lead us not into temptation;
> But deliver us from evil.

Objection 10. "The apostle Paul said in 2 Thessalonians 2:1-3 that our gathering together unto Christ will not be until the coming [*parousia*] of our Lord Jesus Christ. As this gathering together [Rapture] will not occur until the Second Coming of Christ, there will be no removal of the Church until that time. Also, Paul gave two signs before this can happen: 'For that day shall not come, except there come a falling away *first*, and that man of sin be revealed, the son of perdition.'"

We shall quote the verses of this objection in a parallel column with 1 Thessalonians 5:1-9, and point out a few facts to the ordinary reader who may not be able to understand all the technical arguments from the Greek text used by some authors. We doubt that Jesus and the apostles taught in such a manner that only scholars could understand what they meant.

1 Thess. 5:1-9	*2 Thess. 2:1-4*
But of the times and seasons, brethren, ye have no need that I write unto you.	Now we beseech you, brethren, by the coming of our Lord Jesus Christ, and by our gathering together unto him,

For yourselves know perfectly that the day of the Lord so cometh as a thief in the night.

For when they shall say, Peace and safety; then sudden destruction *cometh upon them*, as travail upon a woman with child; and *they* shall not escape.

But ye, brethren, are not in darkness, that that day should overtake you as a thief . . .

For God hath not appointed us to wrath, but to obtain salvation by our Lord Jesus Christ.

That ye be not soon shaken in mind, or be troubled, neither by spirit, nor by word, nor by letter as from us, as that the day of Christ is at hand.

Let no man deceive you by any means; for that day shall not come, except there come a falling away first, and that man of sin be revealed, the son of perdition;

Who opposeth and exalteth himself above all that is called God, or that is worshipped; so that he as God sitteth in the temple of God, shewing himself that he is God.

We observe first that the two columns describe two different events which occur at different periods. The first tells about the beginning of sorrows when "that day" shall come as a thief in the night. The second tells about the end of the sorrows at the time of the Second Coming of Christ.

This should be evident from the fact that there are two different sets of signs in the two passages. In the first, we see the peace-and-safety signs that precede the sudden destruction at the beginning of sorrows. But in the second, we see the falling-away (*apostasia*) and man-of-sin-revealed signs that do not appear until years have passed and the sorrows are well advanced.

If Paul had said that the falling-away and the Antichrist-revealed signs would appear before the beginning of sorrows, then the whole picture would change. It is of crucial importance to understand the signs and to keep them in the proper periods for their appearances. Unless this is done confusion will result, and there is a great deal of it everywhere about the Church and the tribulation.

There isn't anything in column one about salvation from the day of wrath that is inconsistent with what Paul said in column two. Paul's meaning lies deep in the context of column one. God hath appointed us to be saved from the wrath, the sudden destruction, from the birthpangs, and hostile seizure by the thief. Johann Bengel, German scholar of renown, defined the meaning of "salvation" in this verse with these words:

> *Hath appointed . . . to obtain salvation—Salvation* of that kind is intended, by which they who are saved are excepted *from* the multitude of those that perish [his emphasis].[6]

We submit that this interpretation is further justified from the fact that Paul said the destruction "cometh upon *them* . . . and *they* shall not escape." Jesus and Paul used the same words and illustrations in describing this event: "unawares—thief—snare—travail—[*birthpangs*]—escape," etc. (Matt. 24:8; Luke 21:34-36).

In column two Paul said the revelation (disclosure) of Antichrist will be when he sits in the temple —enthrones himself in the temple with the proclamation that he is God. His satanic character will then be known to all—to the Harlot Church (Rev. 17-18), to the Jews, and to all peoples he deceived. This event will occur in the middle of the seven-year period known as Daniel's 70th Week. And it is from this point that power will be "given unto him to continue forty and two months" (Rev. 13:5).

Daniel 9:27 gives further details about the seven-year period:

> And he shall confirm the covenant with many for one week: and in the midst of the week he shall cause the sacrifice and oblation to cease, and for the overspreading of abominations he shall make it desolate, even until the consummation, and that determined shall be poured upon the desolate.

We learn from this that Antichrist shall confirm a covenant with many in Israel, which may be for the protection of them and their land. A big point to see here is that Antichrist is in a ruling position before the seven years begin, and that he has risen to this dominance by conquering any opposition he encounters on the way up. This reminds us again that Paul said his "*coming* is according to the operation of Satan with *all* power and signs and wonders of a lie." [7] The rise of Antichrist will be sensational and spectacular—beyond anything that mortal men ever saw. The world will be astonished at his supreme military power; and in adoration of him, they ask, "Who is able to make war with him?"

We must also observe that there will be another revelation of Antichrist before he deifies himself in the temple. We read about this in Revelation 13:18:

> Here is wisdom. Let him that hath understanding count the number of the beast: for it is the number of a man; and his number is Six hundred threescore and six.

All attempts to connect the number 666 with historical characters have failed—from Nero to Adolph Hitler. The usual fallacy has been to attach to each letter of certain names a numerical value in the Greek alphabet. But the mystery of Antichrist's name will be more than a word puzzle or numerical riddle. The angel indicated to John that the mystery of his name will be discerned only by the "wisdom" and "understanding" of the Holy Spirit.

As Antichrist will be operating in deception and secrecy, it will be necessary for him to keep his identity concealed in his name. But the Holy Spirit will keep the Church alerted and informed. The harlot in Revelation 17:5 also has on her forehead a name of Mystery. With this symbolic title she represents a worldwide system of religion which professes to serve God but is *unfaithful* to Him. Her entire character is summed up in two words: fornication and deception (Rev. 17 and 18).

In Antichrist's name there may be the idea of a secret code number. Dr. George Lamsa also has this idea in his Aramaic translation of Revelation 13:18.[8] Great is the need for the gifts of the Holy Spirit in the end-time Church to guard it against delusions. Wars have been won because of military intelligence, or lost for the lack of it.

Antichrist will need time for his buildup as a world figure before the judgments begin. His preliminary work with signs and wonders will be important to his purpose. Then, this mystery man will convince the nations that only he has the remedy for their dilemma. And all nations, kindreds, and tongues, feeling insecure under shaky governments and fed up with the failures of political systems, will take him as the fulfillment of their dreams of peace and prosperity. But the Church will be protected against his deception by the unveiling of his name.

We know there will be a prior revelation of Antichrist by discernment of his name because when he enthrones himself in the temple, that act alone

will be sufficient to identify him. The earlier iden-
tification will be crucial to the Church.

When Satan is working his mystery to a climax,
God will also be working His. "But in the days of
the voice of the seventh angel, when he shall begin
to sound, the mystery of God should be finished,
as he hath declared to his servants the prophets"
(Rev. 10:7). God's mystery is hidden in the mass
of Old Testament covenant prophecies.

R. B. Girdlestone, Old Testament Hebrew authority, wrote the following in his *The Grammar of Prophecy*:

> There are about 600 quotations from the Old Tes-
> tament to the New, besides constant allusive ref-
> erences. These have been examined and discussed
> from various points of view, but the question now
> before us is simply this: Is there a definite and
> consistent view of Old Testament prediction taken
> by the teachers and writers of the New Testament? [9]

Girdlestone's answer to this question is yes. And
he adds, "The historical events narrated in the Old
Testament are regarded as facts, not as myths, in
the New." Also, we argue that those parts of Old
Testament prophecies fulfilled by Jesus and the apostles were fulfilled literally; therefore, the remaining parts shall likewise be accomplished consistently
and literally. There is a harmonious *wholeness* to
the sense-content of the prophecies in both Testaments.

As the end approaches, God must work on a greater scale because of the large number of prophecies
to be fulfilled. His purpose in our time widens to
worldwide proportions as we see in the present-day
outpouring of the Holy Spirit.

The New Testament Church was launched at Pentecost with amazing acts of the supernatural, and to fully accomplish its appointed mission to the nations during the end time it must never lose its supernatural character because, as never before, Satan is also operating in the realm of the supernatural.

After a brief digression from the above objection, we conclude that Paul's signs about the falling away, and the man of sin revealed, do not conflict with what he said about the salvation of believers from the destruction that shall overtake the unbelievers.

Objection 11. "The Church will escape the wrath of God but not the wrath of man during the tribulation. The day of the Lord, which is the wrath of God, does not begin until chapter 8 of Revelation. The day of wrath does not begin before the time of Rev. 6:17, 'For the great day of his wrath is come; and who shall be able to stand?' "

This objection is similar to Objection 5, so some repetition may be necessary in replying to it.

Revelation 6:17, "For the great day of his wrath is come," does not mean there were not previous judgments, as seen in chapter 6:1-8. "After the Lord has exhausted all his ordinary judgments—the sword, famine, pestilence, and wild beasts—and still sinners are impenitent, the *last great day* of the Lord itself shall come." [10]

God's wrath will be in the judgments from the beginning to the end, increasing in severity and intensity over the entire period until the final fall of "Babylon the great" in Revelation 18. After the seal-plagues, the trumpet-plagues begin, "for in them is filled up [finished] the wrath of God" (Rev. 15:1); and the thunderbolts of His anger move toward a climax with the *"fierceness* of his wrath" in Revelation 16:19.

When Paul wrote about times and seasons in 1 Thessalonians 5:1-3, he clearly stated the period *before* the sudden destruction when he said, "For *when* they shall say, Peace and safety, *then* sudden destruction cometh upon them, as travail upon a woman with child, and they shall not escape." The time "when" they say peace and safety is before the time of "then" sudden destruction cometh. The *when*-time is before the *then*-time when the thief comes and the woman is seized with travail.

Also, Jesus and Paul used the same idea and likeness of birthpangs to represent the beginning of the day of the Lord. Jesus said, "beginning of birthpangs [sorrows]," and Paul said, "as birthpangs [travail] upon a woman with child." So, Jesus and Paul had the day of the Lord starting at the same time. Mid-tribulationists have the day of the Lord starting during the middle of the judgment calamities, and the Post-tribulationists have it at the end of them. But both views are inconsistent with the metaphors of the thief and the pregnant woman.

We need to take a closer look into the meaning of the travail of the pregnant woman because it connects with the rebirth of the earth at the Second Coming of Christ. Jesus, greatest of the prophets, often made astonishing statements about His return to earth. In Matthew 19:28, we read:

> And Jesus said unto them, Verily I say unto you, That ye which have followed me, in the regeneration [new birth] when the Son of man shall sit in the throne of his glory, ye also shall sit upon twelve thrones, judging the twelve tribes of Israel.

This regeneration signifies new creation, new world, born-again earth. It will be the new age when Messiah establishes His kingdom. The messianic

..ingdom was the theme of the prophets and the hope of Israel. And it will be brought to birth by the agonies and sufferings of the catastrophic judgments.

Professor A. T. Robertson, in his comment on the meaning of Matthew 24:8, wrote:

> *The beginning of travail* . . . the word means birth-pangs . . . These woes, says Jesus, are not a proof of the end, but of the beginning.[11]

When Paul wrote in 1 Thessalonians 5:1-9 about times and seasons and about the approaching thief and the destruction, he wrote concerning the times and seasons for "the day of the Lord." This thought follows through in the context. And when he said in verse 9 that God hath not appointed us to wrath, he was still thinking about the wrath of verses 2-3. If he meant that God has appointed us to *part* of the wrath, then Paul, master teacher and inspired apostle, would have carefully specified this fact in his statement.

We conclude that our midtribulation friends have no support for their view that the day of wrath does not begin until the time of Revelation 6:17. The terrors and torments described in verses 1-8 of the same chapter clearly show it is the wrath of "that day." Isn't sudden destruction wrath? Isaiah described the entire period of the judgmental punishments with the word "indignation," and there is no difference between wrath and indignation. As used in Old Testament Hebrew and New Testament Greek, there is no difference of meaning between birth woes and wrath in the relevant prophetic texts.

CHAPTER 11

Summary of Conclusions

1. We began with definitions of the terms, *that day, tribulation, snare,* and *escape.* "That day" was a familiar Old Testament term and it appears frequently in the prophecies, and in these passages *day* and *days* are connected with judgment and are synonyms for judgment. "That day" is a main prophetic term in the Old Testament denoting a period of tribulation for the earth, and this meaning is brought into the New Testament. These terms do not have one meaning in the Old Testament and another in the New. We must see the total meaning, and when all the parts are seen in relation to the whole, the collective sense will be a consistent sense. The difference of meaning that some give to these terms is not supported by the historical usage.

When Jesus warned us to take heed lest that day come upon us unawares, He then said, "For as a snare shall it come on all them that dwell on the face of the whole earth." So "that day" and "snare" refer to the same period of prophetic time. The time will come when the snare will be set and catch its unwary victims. "That day" is a specific term for a definite period of time.

2. For the meaning of "tribulation" (*thlipsis*), we cited the authoritative Arndt & Gingrich lexicon. It signifies "pressure, oppression, distress, afflictions ... (it is used) of a woman's birthpangs, John 16:21."

Jesus said the travailing woman knows that "her hour is come." And in Matthew 24:8 He spoke of "the beginning of birthpangs." Paul used the same word when he wrote in 1 Thessalonians 5:3, "For when they say, Peace and safety; then sudden destruction cometh upon them, as birthpangs upon a woman with child; and they shall not escape."

In problems of interpretation, it sometimes helps if we can find a *unifying factor*. There is unity and harmony in the use that Jesus and Paul made with birthpangs. Both spoke about the same event and had it occurring at the same time. Jesus connected the beginning of travail with that day, and Paul likewise. So, the beginning of the travail is the beginning of the tribulation.

3. The word *snare* was defined by the lexicons as a trap used by Satan to allure and ensnare. It is used of the sudden judgments to come upon the world in that day (Luke 21:34-36). It is also a tempting bribe offered by Satan to lead men into unsuspecting danger. Thayer, citing Luke 21:35, said a snare is "whatever brings peril, loss, destruction: of a sudden and unexpected deadly peril."

There are many references to snares in the Old Testament, and Jesus used the word as being familiar to His hearers. The term "that day" also seems to have been familiar to them. In both Testaments, the words "unawares" and "deception" are sometimes associated with snares.

4. We saw that the Greek word for escape is *ekpheugo*, and that it signifies: "to get free from; to flee out of; to evade a captor; to get safely away from danger." This meaning can be verified from standard sources which also specify escape from the tribulation of Luke 21:36. We gave references for three sources.

Several texts were also used to illustrate the above definition. In Psalm 124:7, "Our soul is escaped as a bird out of the snare of the fowlers; the snare is broken, and we are escaped." In 2 Corinthians 11:32-33, Paul told about the trap set for him at the gates of Damascus. He was let down over the wall in a basket and was safely whisked away from those who intended to kill him.

Jesus used the word *escape* in a context about the dangers of the snare in that day, and admonished us to pray that we be worthy to get safely out of those snares.

5. Paul used our Lord's favorite illustration about the thief, and like Jesus, he taught that the day of the Lord will come as a thief in the night. If we could know when the thief would come, we could know when the day of the Lord will begin. Paul taught that we could watch for the approaching thief when the world is saying, "Peace and safety." From all the signs about the day of the Lord, Paul specified two.

A world peace plan that works will be a temporary reality before the day begins, because one of the first judgments of that day will be "to take peace from the earth" (Rev. 6:4).

In 1 Thessalonians 5:1-9, Paul used a set of contrasts. Two ideas are brought into sharp contrast by placing them side by side. "They" shall be overtaken by the thief, and, "sudden destruction *cometh upon them* ... and they shall not escape [*ekphugosin*]. But *ye*, brethren, are not in darkness, that that day should overtake you as a thief." And, as we are not overtaken by the thief, then we shall escape the destruction that comes as a thief. We shall escape all that the others do not escape.

We showed that the Greek word for overtake (*katalambano*) signifies to take possession of by seizure—"to seize with hostile intent; to lay hold of so as to possess as one's own." Jesus used the same word in John 12:35-36, "Walk while you have the light, lest darkness come upon [overtake] you." *Overtake* emphasizes "taking hold suddenly and with force."

Paul added that God hath not appointed us to the wrath of that day when the destruction cometh, but that we are appointed to salvation—to be saved from the wrath.

Salvation (*soteria*) is a generic or comprehensive word with wide meaning in the Scriptures. It signifies much more than the saving from sin. In about one-third of the New Testament references it signifies deliverance from danger, disease, and demon possession. It expresses physical safety and wellbeing. We quoted the authoritative Arndt & Gingrich lexicon:

> Salvation [soteria] signifies to "bring out safely from a situation fraught with mortal danger." it is used, "of the evil days of the last tribulation."

Paul used salvation twice with the meaning of deliverance from the tribulation wrath. He illustrated this with the armed soldier having on the breastplate of faith and love and the helmet of salvation. These were symbols of protection and victorious warfare.

Salvation and *escape* sometimes have similar meanings in the New Testament. In Acts 27:44, after the shipwreck, they were saved with boards and broken pieces of the ship. "And so it came to pass, that they escaped all safe to land." The word *escaped* here means to be saved by getting safely out of danger. In "escape" the idea of *danger* is to be emphasized.

In 2 Peter 2:5, God "saved Noah" from the flood. The word here means "to preserve alive." And in verse 7, Peter said God "delivered" Lot from Sodom's judgment, and this word "is largely synonymous with *sozo*, to save" (Vine). Noah was safely in the ark before the flood came, and Lot was safely out of Sodom before the fire fell.

In the conversation between Lot and the delivering angel (Gen. 19:15-22), the word "escape" was used five times. The angel warned him to hasten and "escape to the mountain, lest thou be consumed." And Lot spoke of the angel as "saving my life." His escape was his salvation.

In commenting on the meaning of *salvation* in 1 Thessalonians 5:9, Johann Bengel, highly respected by Greek scholars, wrote:

> *To obtain salvation—Salvation* of that kind is intended by which they who are saved are excepted *from* the multitude of those that perish.[1]

Various translators also give similar meanings to verse 9 in their translations.

> For God has not destined us to incur His anger. (Weymouth)

> For God did not choose us to condemn us. (Phillips)
>
> For God has not destined us to the terrors of judgment. (*New English Bible*)

From the meaning of the Greek text, and by fair rules of interpretation, we conclude there is a connection of thought in verses 1-9; therefore, Paul clearly stated that we shall be saved from the wrath of "the day of the Lord"; saved from the sudden destruction of "that day"; saved from the birthpangs; and saved from hostile seizure by the thief (vv. 2-4).

6. We saw in Revelation 3:10 that Christ promised those who keep His word that He also will keep them from "the hour of temptation which shall come upon all the world, to try them that dwell upon the earth." This is similar to Christ's statement in Luke 21:35, "For as a snare shall it come on all them that dwell on the face of the whole earth." In both places Jesus spoke about the final world trial that will test the nations.

We quoted New Testament authorities who said that this all-nations trial shall be of no ordinary kind, that it will precede the coming of Christ, and that it is immediately connected with "I come quickly."

Jesus and the apostles drew warnings from history. In Deuteronomy 4:34 the plagues are called "the temptations of Egypt." "The hour of temptation" is the appointed season of affliction, "*the* sore temptation coming on," "the great tribulation" before Christ's second coming.

We connected the word *temptation* in Revelation 3:10 with Peter's use of the word in 2 Peter 2:4-9 and saw that in both places it has a prophetic meaning: "The Lord knoweth how to deliver the godly *out of* temptations. . . . "

Peter's sentences (4-9) are another unit-of-thought passage. Peter, like Jesus, used the Noah-Lot comparisons. He began his thought in verse 4 and ended it in verse 9. And he said the judgments in the times of Noah and Lot were "examples," or object lessons. The ungodly were not "spared," but Noah and Lot were. And as God delivered Noah and Lot when their generations were put on trial, so also He knoweth how to deliver the godly out of the coming trial.[2]

We have been repetitious on several points. This could not be avoided. Jesus repeated some truths again and again. And Peter said he was purposely repetitious (1 Pet. 1:12; 3:1). We shall now see that our main line of argument runs through the five passages that we have considered, and that there is repetition and unity of thought in them.

(1) Luke 21:34-36: We must take heed lest our hearts be overcharged with the pleasures and cares of this life, and that day come upon us unawares.

We must watch and pray always that we shall be worthy to escape all the things about to come to pass in that day upon the entire earth.

(2) 1 Thessalonians 5:1-9: Paul taught that God has not appointed us to the wrath of that day. But we are appointed to be saved from it.

(3) 2 Peter 2:1-9: Peter drew warnings from past judgments in the days of Noah and Lot, and said they were examples of the coming judgments. God delivered Noah and Lot, and He knows how to deliver the godly out of the coming world temptation.

(4) Revelation 3:10: Christ again spoke about an event that will be a special trial for the inhabited earth. And to all who keep His word, He promised to keep them out of it.

(5) Luke 17:28-33: "Remember Lot's wife." Jesus

selected this woman as a special example for many who will not escape the *dangers* of the last days. There are many like her in churches everywhere today. And Jesus was sounding a warning about the judgment of that day when He told us to remember her. She was escaping Sodom's doom with an angel holding her hand, but she looked back and was lost. The meaning of the object lesson is that, if we don't look back, we shall escape the judgment, as she did not. If we continue to look ahead and move forward, we shall "preserve" our lives, as she did not. Lot's wife was lost while she was being saved.

On the meaning of the word "temptation" in Revelation 3:10, we have seen an interesting development in our time with the Arab oil embargo. A few small Arab countries have caused international upheaval and economic havoc with their embargo. And they have used it with much effect to force European and Asian nations to their side against Israel. Their oil has been a powerful temptation to strong nations.

The time hasn't yet come for the mark of the beast, but we wonder what the result would have been if the Arabs had insisted that the crippled nations, desperate for oil, must first accept a certain mark or stamp before they could buy it? The Arab world is an Antichrist-world. Could the embargo be a preview of bigger things to come?

7. In the chapter on the signs that precede the tribulation, when Jesus illustrated this with the trees, He said that when they put forth leaves, "ye know that summer is nigh." The point here is that we can know when the summer is near. So also shall it be before the day begins. It is important to dis-

tinguish between the signs that appear *before* the day begins and *after* it begins. It is in these first-signs or preliminary events that we are primarily interested.

Hebrews 10:25 also says that we can "see the day approaching." Many New Testament scholars agree that this text speaks of the signs of the times that will appear before the day of the Lord.[3]

> *The day drawing nigh* . . . the Second Coming of Christ. (Robertson)
> *Ye see* . . . from the signs of the times. (Bengel)
> It appeals at once to the watchfulness and discernment of the readers as regards the signs of the times. (Alford)

Before the destruction of Jerusalem in A.D. 70 the Christians saw the signs that Christ had given and escaped. And if what we read in the records is true, the Christians escaped in A.D. 68. The siege by Titus was a long one.

Jesus said as there were preflood signs in Noah's day, so also there shall be pretribulation signs. This was also true in the days of Lot. Two of the preliminary signs Jesus mentioned were "wars and commotions," and He added, "Be not terrified: for these things must first come to pass." There have always been wars, but never the threat of nuclear wars. Military leaders have warned about the terrifying possibility of hundreds of millions killed in a single attack. We have also been warned of the possibility that terrorists may blow up our nuclear power plants across America. England and America are building many more. Terrorists have circulated blueprints of the atomic bomb. How did they get them?

There have always been commotions but never like those that will precede "that day." Commotions signify disorders, tumults, riots, anarchy, and conditions that cause panic. Add all this to the possibility of nuclear war and we understand why Jesus told us to "be not terrified." The nations have intelligence experts on the alert, prepared to push the panic button. It surely would be terrifying if we did not escape it. There isn't anything in the past comparable to the dangerous world situation that is being set up today for Antichrist.

The apostles wrote about the mystery of Antichrist and the mystery of the Harlot Church. These two are working together in a world-coordinated system to produce the necessary conditions for the appearance of Antichrist. Observers report that world leaders are in confusion and see no way out of their dilemmas. One cabled: "Europe is living on crises."

Crucial times are especially dangerous because Satan has special devices to take advantage of them. "In the last days perilous times shall come." There have always been perilous times, but the final seasons will be the worse, and Satan will have special forces working that are adapted to the end of the age. Jesus gave greater stress to the end-time deceptions than to any other.

The European Common Market has its problems. And industrial nations, anxious to protect their foreign markets, have been weakened by competitive nations who seek to strengthen their trading positions. The result has been a world chain reaction of competitive reprisals.

The world-trade sign is taking shape. International trade is important to world prosperity because it is related to the economic and monetary problems of the nations. Even the United States with all its natural resources is dependent on other nations for large imports of basic raw materials.

Dramatic changes are in the making. A unified Europe will come, and a booming international trade. The rush is on in American and foreign ship-yards to build the superships and supertankers. The big industrial nations say they cannot get them fast enough. Shipping experts say this is "the supertrans-port era." For more details read Revelation 18.

From all the signs, Paul specified two—peace and prosperity. Peace is the most pressing problem con-fronting the United Nations. For years there have been peace talks by world leaders, the Pope, and ecumenical leaders. At this writing there seems to be hope of peace in the Mid East. But news reports say thousands of soldiers and thousands of civilians have been killed in the Far East since the peace agreement was signed there. The explosive situation between Russia and China is frequently at flash-point.

No other generation has seen the signs develop-ing together as we see them today. No other genera-tion has seen the restored Israeli State, nor the signs of "uniworld" and "unichurch," nor Joel's sign of the global outpouring of the Holy Spirit and world evangelization. "And this gospel of the kingdom shall be preached in all the world for a witness unto all nations; and then shall the end come" (Matt. 24:14).

8. After the chapter on signs we then considered Peter's statement that "one day is with the Lord as a thousand years, and a thousand years as one day." And this was said in a context about the "last days."

We saw previously that there are about 600 Old Testament quotations in the New Testament besides numerous allusive references. Some of these were literally fulfilled by Christ at His first coming but they were partial fulfillments. The completed fulfillments at His second coming shall likewise be literal. How could the first part be literal and the second nonliteral?

> In examining the forms of prophetic thought in Scripture we find none so common as the expression of the future in terms borrowed from the historic past.
>
> Literal, if possible, is, I believe, the only maxim that will carry you right through the Word of God from Genesis to Revelation.[4]

Girdlestone also said (page 69) that "future events are clothed in language borrowed from the past...." The future is expressed in terms of the past as seen in the Old Testament.

With so much prophecy to be literally fulfilled as the end of the age draws near, we may think that long periods of time will be necessary to accomplish this. But Peter said that God can do in one day what He has not done for a thousand years.

When God let Isaiah see one of His future projects, and the rapidity by which it should be done, the prophet was astonished and exclaimed in amazement:

> Who hath heard such a thing? who hath seen such things? Shall the earth be made to bring forth in one day? or a nation born at once? (Isa. 66:8)

This is one of the many events in God's prophetic plan as the end approaches: things unheard of, things never seen before, and the speed by which it shall be done will stagger the nations. We suggested before that if anyone thinks our statements about world changes are farfetched and exaggerated, let him read Dr. Toffler's nonreligious book, *Future Shock*.

With such a large number of prophecies to be fulfilled in a short space of time, this project must be carried out and terminated by a rapid succession of events. Our Lord said it would all be done in the lifetime of the generation living at the time of final fulfillment. The severity and rapidity of the judgments would destroy all flesh unless God shortens the judgment period.

Paul, also writing about the speedy completion of God's dealings with the nations, said, "For he will finish the work, and cut it short in righteousness: because a short work will the Lord make upon the earth."

Jesus stressed the swiftness of the ancient judgments when the merrymakers were surprised with the sudden catastrophes. So also shall it be in that day. When God destroys the dream-world of peace and plenty that apostate nations shall build, they will be overwhelmed by the suddenness of it. "Alas, alas, that great city Babylon, that mighty city! for in one hour is thy judgment come . . . for in one hour so great riches is come to nought."

9. On the meaning of "worthy to escape," we learned that *worthy* signifies to have worth or value. It does not mean that we are saved by works or that we can earn our salvation. We are not worthy in the sense that Christ is worthy. If we could save ourselves, then Christ died in vain.

John the Baptist told his converts to prove their repentance with fruits worthy of repentance. Evidence of sincerity was also required by Jesus and the apostles. These fruit works are not the change of heart but the righteous acts which result from it, and by proving our love for Christ we have spiritual worth.

True faith will manifest itself in righteous, visible actions. "Let your light so shine before men, that they may see your good works, and glorify your Father which is in heaven" (Matt. 5:16). Jesus and the apostles were united on the truth that only those who produce fruits of righteousness are genuine believers. This truth runs throughout the New Testament. People can claim what they will, but the Bible requires proof.

Jesus was severe in His requirements for discipleship, and with strong emphasis He said that if anyone loved anything more than Him, he was not worthy of Him. This is repeated three times in two verses (Matt. 10:37-38).

Paul told the Thessalonians that the persecutions they endured "were a manifest token of the righteous judgment of God, that ye may be counted worthy of the kingdom of God." Trials are the means by which God proves faith, and it is proven faith that is "more precious than of gold that perisheth," because it has spiritual value. There are many contrasts in the Bible between persons of worth and those worthless. We see so much in churches today that is cheap and worthless, and according to Paul (1 Cor. 3:11-15), such works will not survive the fiery test of the judgment seat when Christ comes.

Paul wrote about faith and works in Ephesians 2:8-10.

> For by grace are ye saved through faith; and that not of yourselves: it is the gift of God. (v. 8)
> Not of works, lest any man should boast. (v. 9)
> For we are his workmanship, created in Christ Jesus unto good works, which God hath before ordained that we should walk in them. (v. 10)

All our lifetime we have heard many quote verses

8-9, but not once did they quote verse 10. And verse 10 is part of Paul's thought in verses 8-9. To quote 8-9 and omit 10 is to quote unfairly because "for" (*gar*) is a connective and it is explanatory of what follows in verse 10. We do not express Paul's complete thought unless we quote the three verses together. These verses are another unit of thought.

God's greatest miracle was not the creation of the physical universe but His creating "children of wrath" (Eph. 2:3) into sons of God. Salvation does not originate in ourselves but in God's divine decree, and it is therefore His free gift. But good works or righteous acts were also part of the creative decree to be fulfilled in us, and that "we should walk [live] in them."

To create a people without this righteousness was not the predestined [ordained] purpose, and without righteous acts God's purpose is not accomplished in us. The Greek word for workmanship is *poiema*, and it denotes "a product" or "that which is made." It is grammatically correct to say that God purposed to make spiritual products in whom He could create righteous acts. Christ "gave himself for us, that he might redeem us from all iniquity, *and* purify unto himself a peculiar people, zealous of good works." My Greek Testament reads: " . . . and might cleanse for himself a people [of] his own possession, zealous of good works" (Titus 2:14, Nestles' text).

The Lord's inheritance is His people. We quoted from three texts to show that genuine believers are rich in faith, rich in good works, and rich towards God, and these virtues are "in the sight of God of great price." These worthies are God's predestinated ones, elected to salvation, and they shall never perish. Worthy is the Lamb who was crucified on Skull Hill to make it possible.

10. Fine linen is the righteousness of the saints. We cited Nestle, Thayer, Cremer, Abbott-Smith, Vincent, Robertson, and others to show that "righteousness" in this text signifies *righteous deeds.*

From all the fabrics in the world the Lord selected fine linen to represent His bridal church. The garment symbol is prominent in the Bible, and it has deep spiritual meaning. God's relation to His people is expressed in terms of marriage, and this provides the most intimate basis of union with them.

Paul gave symbolic expression to the undefiled character of the Church when he said it will be presented to Christ as a chaste virgin. Undefiled by other lovers, she is a model of holiness.

"His wife hath made herself ready." This is the central truth of all New Testament teaching—"to make ready a people prepared for the Lord." An analysis of all that Jesus taught about His coming shows that preparation for it was the point most emphasized. The wedding robe is the Bridegroom's gift to the Bride, but she has to put it on.

The beating, soaking, washing, and separation of the flax is a picture of continuous and thorough preparation. The weaver gives it his workmanship, and then passes it on for final inspection.

Paul said the bridal union of Christ and the Church is a great mystery in which the two become one. Christ's divine life operates in the Church and combines with faith and love of the Bride, and this results in righteous deeds and actions. And the apostle John said that without such deeds and actions one is not righteous.

All the attributes of God are summed up in one

word: *righteous*. This word comprehends all His moral excellence. The moral character of the espoused Church is also summed up in one word: *righteousness*. Why is it that this truth, so much emphasized in Scripture, is so much neglected in the churches today?

> Little children, let no man deceive you: he that doeth righteousness is righteous, even as he is righteous.
> He that committeth sin is of the devil. (1 John 3:7-8)

In reply to various objections, we have stated that our position of pretribulation escape does not conflict with the posttribulation rapture of our opponents. In other words, our escape texts are not inconsistent with their rapture texts. And this applies to the texts used by both midtribulation and posttribulation exponents.

But on the other hand, the interpretation they put on the rapture texts is inconsistent with the escape texts. And their interpretation violates the *rule of consistency* which says: "An interpretation must not only be consistent with one text; it must not be inconsistent with other texts."

Our Lord told us to pray that we shall be accounted worthy to escape the tribulation events He described in the Olivet Discourse. It has been our purpose to prove what this escape means. We have not entered into the question about *how* we shall escape, but only that we shall.

Peter said, that the Lord knew *how* to deliver the godly out of judgment, as He knew how to deliver Noah and Lot. He knew how to deliver the Christians in the destruction of Jerusalem in A.D. 70, and He will know how to deliver the 144,000 with the seal of the living God. He will also know how to deliver others from the tribulation wrath by providing for them "a place prepared of God" (Rev. 12:6). As these deliverances will be provided *after* the tribulation begins, how much more will God deliver those who shall be worthy to escape *before* it begins?

We also replied to another objection: "Christians have suffered tribulation through nineteen centuries of church history. Why then should they be exempted from the tribulation of the day of the Lord?"

Our reply to the previous objection will also cover this one. Various groups will escape God's day of tribulation. There is tribulation that all must endure. Jesus said, "In the world ye shall have tribulation," and Paul said that "we must through much tribulation enter into the kingdom of God." But let us observe a clear distinction that Paul makes between the tribulation we are appointed to and that which we are not appointed to. In 1 Thessalonians 3:2-3, Paul wrote:

> We . . . sent Timotheus, our brother, and minister of God, and our fellowlabourer in the gospel of Christ, to establish you, and to comfort you concerning your faith:
>
> That no man should be moved by these afflictions [Gk. *tribulations*]: for yourselves know that we are appointed thereunto.

All are "appointed" to *these* tribulations, but a little later in the same epistle when Paul wrote about the tribulation of God's day of wrath, he said:

> For God hath not appointed us to wrath, but to obtain salvation by our Lord Jesus Christ. (5:9)

So there is tribulation to which we are appointed and that to which we are not appointed. Could Paul have been more specific in the difference between the two?

We have also replied to an objection by midtribulation exponents who argue that the Church will not escape the wrath of man but will escape the wrath of God. They argue that the first part of the judgments is the wrath of man and the Church must endure this; but the wrath of God does not begin until Revelation 6:17, "For the great day of his wrath is come, and who shall be able to stand?" It is at this time that the Church will be raptured, they say, and not at the beginning of the tribulation period.

To this we argue that the entire judgment period is a day of God's wrath. When Jesus spoke about the "beginning of sorrows," He meant the beginning of God's wrath. The beginning, middle, and end of the judgments is God's anger or wrath. The day begins when "sudden destruction cometh upon them," and this destruction is God's wrath.

God's anger increases over the entire judgment period until the fall of Babylon in Revelation 18. After the seal-plagues, the trumpet-plagues begin, "for in them is filled up [finished] the wrath of God" (Rev. 15:1), and the judgments are climaxed with the "fierceness of his wrath" (Rev. 16:19). The beginning of sorrows is the starting point of God's wrath. "Great day of his wrath" doesn't mean preceding judgments are not wrath.

Another objection stated that we are not to watch and pray for signs in order to escape the tribulation because the Lord said He would come as a thief in the night. And the thief illustration in Revelation 16:15 indicates it will be at the Second Coming that Christ will come as a thief.

In answer to this we showed that the Lord will not come as a thief at His second coming because after the day of the Lord begins, the time of His second coming can be closely calculated. When Satan is cast down to earth before the Second Coming, he knows that he has but a "short time." Satan then mobilizes the world armies at Armageddon to oppose Christ at His coming in Jerusalem; and they are there, ready and prepared, to resist Christ at His coming. How, then, could Christ come as a thief at His appearing?

Also, Jesus said frightful signs would precede His appearance at Jerusalem. There will be signs in the sun, moon, and stars, and fearful events will indicate the end is near. But no such signs will appear before the day of the Lord begins when the sudden destruction strikes the world "unawares."

Jesus specified the fact there will be no secrecy about His second coming:

> Wherefore, if they shall say unto you . . . behold, he is in the secret chambers; believe it not.
>
> For as the lightning cometh out of the east, and shineth even unto the west; so shall also the coming of the Son of man be. (Matt. 24:26-27)

He will not come as a thief in the darkness but as the lightning flash from east to west—to be seen and recognized by all the world.

For our last point in this summary we refer to the posttribulation argument from Matthew 24:13. In this text Jesus was speaking about the tribulation judgments, and said, "But he that shall endure unto the end, the same shall be saved." It is argued from this that none escape the tribulation, but that all must endure unto the end of it.

If Jesus had said in Luke 21:36, "Watch and pray,

that ye may be accounted worthy to endure all these things unto the end," then this would have been strong evidence against our position. But He did not say that. He said the very opposite. "Escape" and "endure" are two different words.

In reply to a previous objection we showed that others escape the judgments after the day of the Lord begins. But endurance unto the end will be necessary for some, and many will be martyred.

We conclude by asking the reader to consider three texts in which Jesus used the same word for "temptation" (*peirasmos*).

> And lead us not into temptation, but deliver us from evil. (Matt. 6:13)
> Watch ye and pray, lest ye enter into temptation. (Mark 14:38)

(The word "lest" here signifies "that not." So what Jesus said was, Watch ye and pray, *that* ye *not* enter into temptation.)

> Because thou hast kept the word of my patience,
> I also will keep thee from the hour of temptation,
> which shall come upon all the world, to try them
> that dwell upon the earth. (Rev. 3:10)

In this text Christ spoke of the *time* of the world temptation. And Paul, in 1 Thessalonians 5:1-3, wrote about the *time* of the sudden destruction, illustrating this with the pregnant woman whose time has come when she is seized with birthpangs. Jesus and Paul were not speaking about tribulation in the general sense but in a special and future sense.

The day of the Lord is the total tribulation period with specific points of time indicated by Jesus with "beginning" of sorrows and the "end" of the sorrows. That day embraces the total period of the final tribulation. "In the last days perilous [dangerous] times shall come." It will be a time of terror and danger for which there are no precedents in history.

In support of these views we previously cited standard Greek authorities, and we add another, the *Theological Dictionary of the New Testament*, edited by Kittel and Friedrich.[5]

An interpreter must not only be concerned with definition and usage but also with the theological meanings of the prophecies. But definition and usage are important because the theological must be derived from the grammatical. There is much about God as revealed in the prophecies that we have not dealt with because our subject deals primarily with the escape of the Church from the tribulation period.

We conclude that God's will is revealed in the prophecies, and that He has put in His word a power that shall one day bring it to pass, every jot and tittle. Many unbelievers look on the earth mission of Jesus as a failure. When asked why Jews do not accept Jesus as Messiah, our Jewish guide in Israel replied, "Jesus did not bring us peace." But the supposed failure of Jesus in human affairs is explained in His words to Pilate: "My kingdom is not of this world."

Nine Rules of Interpretation

Interpretation has been defined as "the science of meaning." Over a period of many years I searched the world's foremost authorities on this science, both in theology and law, and found these nine basic rules universally accepted in the arena of logic and evidence during the past 2500 years.

They are found in the reasonings of Socrates and Aristotle who have profoundly influenced interpretation to the present day. They are also found in the writings of the church fathers, from Irenaeus in the second century, to the Reformation theologians. They were used in the great doctrinal debates of the theologians from the Council of Nice (324 A.D.) to the Council of Trent (1545-1563). But in many of these councils a clear definition of terms was avoided and the rules often violated. The result was confusion, and Paul said that "God is not the author of confusion."

The doctrinal calamities of nineteen centuries of church history were violations of these rules, and the same is true of all false doctrines in Christendom today.

Professor John Wigmore, a foremost legal authority, called some interpreters "word magicians" because of their attempts to make words mean what they wanted them to mean. Many false doctrines could not stand without the support of word-magic. Many Bible doctrines are expressed in a single word or term, and if we do not get the definition right, we do not get the doctrine right. A false start will surely lead to a false conclusion. In theology as in law, you can win or lose on the meaning of a single word.

Exact rules are needed for an exact result. Paul told us to "prove all things," and he used these rules of interpretation. So also did Jesus and the other apostles, and they confounded their opponents with them. Every interpreter thinks he is right, but not every interpreter can prove he is right. "A false interpretation will inevitably betray itself" (Trench).

When conflicting interpretations are claimed for a scripture, the one that best satisfies the rules will be the safest to adopt. Evidence must be based on rational grounds of everyday logic, and logic is defined as "reasonable argument." But there can be no reasonable argument without compliance to universally accepted rules of interpretation.

All of the rules listed below are actual quotations from works of scholars of the past and of the present.

1. Rule of Definition

"Any study of Scripture . . . must begin with a study of words." (*Protestant Biblical Interpretation*, Ramm, Bernard, p. 129. W. A. Wilde Co., Boston. 1956.)

"Define your terms and then keep to the terms defined." (*The Structural Principles of the Bible*, Marsh, F. E., p. 1, Kregel Publications.)

"In the last analysis, our theology finds its solid foundation only in the grammatical sense of Scripture. The interpreter should . . . conscientiously abide by the plain meaning of the words." (*Principles of Biblical Interpretation*, Berkhof, pp. 74-75, Baker Book House, 1960.)

"The Bible writers could not coin new words since they would not be understood, and were therefore forced to use those already in use. The content of meaning in these words is not to be determined by each individual expositor . . . to do so would be a method of interpretation [that is] a most vicious thing." (*Studies in the Vocabulary of the Greek New Testament*, Wuest, Kenneth, pp. 30-37, Eerdmans Pub. Co., 1945.)

"[The author] confines the definitions strictly to their literal or idiomatic force; which, after all, will be found to form the best, and indeed the only safe and solid basis for theological deductions of any kind." (Young's *Analytical Concordance to the Bible*, Prefatory Note.)

2. Rule of Usage

"The whole Bible may be regarded as written for 'the Jew first,' and its words and idioms ought to be rendered according to Hebrew usage." (*Synonyms of the Old Testament*, Girdlestone, R. B., p. 14.)

"Christ then accepted the usage He found existing. He did not alter it." (*Pulpit Commentary*, "Matthew," V. 1, xxv, old edition.)

144

"Jesus of Nazareth was a Jew, spoke to and moved among Jews in Palestine. . . . He spoke first and directly to the Jews, and His words must have been intelligible to them. . . It was absolutely necessary to view that Life and Teaching in all its surroundings of place, society, popular life. . . . This would form not only the frame in which to set the picture of the Christ, but the very background of the picture itself." (*The Life and Times of Jesus the Messiah*, Edersheim, Alfred, V. 1, xii, Eerdmans Pub. Co., 1953.)

"In interpreting very many phrases and histories of the New Testament, it is not so much worth what we think of them from notions of our own . . . as in what sense these things were understood by the hearers and lookers on, according to the usual custom and vulgar dialect of the nation." (*Bishop Lightfoot*, quoted in *The Vocabulary of the Greek New Testament*, xii. Moulton & Mulligan, Eerdmans Pub. Co., 1959.)

3. Rule of Context

"Many a passage of Scripture will not be understood at all without the help afforded by the context; for many a sentence derives all its point and force from the connection in which it stands." (*Biblical Hermeneutics*, Terry, M. S., p. 117, 1896.)

"[Bible words] must be understood according to the requirements of the context." (Thayer's *A Greek-English Lexicon of the New Testament*, p. 97.)

"Every word you read must be understood in the light of the words that come before and after it." (*How To Make Sense*, Flesch, Rudolph, p. 51, Harper & Brothers, 1954.)

"[Bible words] when used out of context . . . can prove almost anything. [Some interpreters] twist them . . . from a natural to a non-natural sense." (Irenaeus, second-century church father, quoted in *Inspiration and Interpretation*, p. 50, Eerdmans Pub. Co., 1957.)

"The meaning must be gathered from the context." (*Encyclopaedia Britannica*, "Interpretation of Documents," V. 8, p. 912, 1959.)

4. Rule of Historical Background

"Even the general reader must be aware that some knowledge of Jewish life and society at the time is requisite for the understanding of the Gospel history." (*The Life and Times of Jesus the Messiah*, Edersheim, Alfred, V. 1, xiii, Eerdmans Pub. Co., 1953.)

"The moment the student has in his mind what was in the mind of the author or authors of the Biblical books when these were written, he has interpreted the thought of Scripture. . . . If he adds anything of his own, it is not exegesis." (*International Standard Bible Encyclopedia*, V. 3, p. 1489, 1952.)

"Theological interpretation and historical investigation can never be separated from each other. . . . The strictest historical . . . scrutiny is an indispensable discipline to all Biblical theology." (*A Theological Word Book of the Bible*, 30 scholars, Preface, Macmillan Co., 1958.)

"I have said enough to show the part which the study of history necessarily plays in the intelligent study of the law as it is today. . . . Our only interest in the past is for the light it throws upon the present." (U.S. Supreme Court Justice Oliver Wendell Holmes,

Jr., 1902-1932, quoted in *The World of Law*, V. 2, p. 630, Simon & Schuster, 1960.)

5. Rule of Logic

"Interpretation is merely logical reasoning." (*Encyclopedia Americana*, V. 15, p. 261, 1953.)

"The use of reason in the interpretation of Scripture is everywhere to be assumed. The Bible comes to us in the forms of human language, and appeals to our reason . . . it invites investigation and it is to be interpreted as we interpret any other volume by a rigid application of the same laws of language, and the same grammatical analysis." (*Biblical Hermeneutics*, Terry, M. S., p. 25, 1895.)

"What is the control we use to weed out false theological speculation? Certainly the control is logic and evidence . . . interpreters who have not had the sharpening experience of logic . . . may have improper notions of implication and evidence. Too frequently such a person uses a basis of appeal that is a notorious violation of the laws of logic and evidence." (*Protestant Biblical Interpretation*, Ramm, Bernard, pp. 151-153, W. A. Wilde Co., 1956.)

"It is one of the most firmly established principles of law in England and in America that "a law means exactly what it says, and is to be interpreted and enforced exactly as it reads." This is just as good a principle for interpreting the Bible as for interpreting law." (*The Importance and Value of Proper Bible Study*, Torrey, R. A., pp. 67-70, Moody Press, 1921.)

Charles G. Finney, lawyer and theologian, is widely considered the greatest theologian and most successful revivalist since apostolic times. He was often in sharp conflict with the theologians of his day because they violated these rules of interpretation. Finney said he interpreted a Bible passage as he "would have understood the same or like passage in a law book." (*Autobiography*, pp. 42-43.)

Finney stressed the need for definition and logic in theology and said the Bible must be understood on "fair principles of interpretation such as would be admitted in a court of justice." (*Systematic Theology*, Preface, ix.)

6. Rule of Precedent

"We must not violate the known usage of a word and invent another for which there is no precedent." (*The Greek New Testament for English Readers*, Alford, Henry, p. 1098, Moody Press.)

"The professional ability of lawyers in arguing a question of law, and the judges in deciding it, is thus chiefly occupied with a critical study of previous cases, in order to determine whether the previous cases really support some alleged doctrine." (*Introduction to the Study of Law*, p. 40, Woodruff, E. H., 1898.)

"The first thing he [the judge] does is to compare the case before him with precedents. . . . Back of precedents are the basic judicial conceptions which are postulates of judicial reasoning, and farther back are the habits of life, the institutions of society, in which those conceptions had their origin. . . . Precedents have so covered the ground that they fix the point of departure from which the labor of the judge begins. Almost invariably, his first step is to examine and compare them. It is a process of search, comparison, and little more." (U.S. Supreme Court Justice Benjamin Cardozo, 1932-1938, *The Nature of the Judicial Process*, quoted in *The World of Law*, V. 2, p. 671, Simon & Schuster, 1960.)

7. Rule of Unity

"[It is] fundamental to a true interpretation of the Scripture, viz., that the parts of a document, law, or instrument are to be construed with reference to the significance of the whole." (Dean Abbot, *Commentary on Matthew*, Interpretation, p. 31.)

"Where a transaction is carried out by means of several documents so that together they form part of a single whole, these documents are read together as one. . . . [They are to be so read] that, that construction is to be preferred which will render them consistent." (*Interpretation of Documents*, Sir Roland Burrows, p. 49, Butterworth & Co., London, 1946.)

8. Rule of Inference

In the law of evidence, an inference is a fact reasonably implied from another fact. It is a logical consequence. It is a process of reasoning. It derives a conclusion from a given fact or premise. It is the deduction of one proposition from another proposition. It is a conclusion drawn from evidence. An inferential fact or proposition, although not expressly stated, is sufficient to bind. This principle of interpretation is upheld by law courts. (Jesus proved the resurrection of the dead to the unbelieving Sadducees by this rule (Matt. 22:31, 32). See *Encyclopaedia Britannica*, V. 6, p. 615 (1952) and *Black's Law Dictionary*, p. 436, Fourth Edition, West Pub. Co., 1951.)

9. Rule of Consistency

"An interpretation must not only be consistent with one text; it must not be inconsistent with other texts." (Quoted by Chairman Samuel Ervin at the U.S. Senate Watergate Investigation, Washington, D.C., June, 1973.)

Biblical prophecy is one and the same subject in the Bible, although it is divided into two parts—the Old and New Testaments. But both parts have one consistent sense throughout. There is unity of definition and meaning in prophetic terms and symbols.

We must read the total meaning in the light of the total revelation in both Testaments. The meaning of a particular part or expression will agree with the total sense. Each part is harmoniously related to other parts, and a true interpretation will not set one text at variance with other texts. The collective sense will be a consistent sense. "The whole Bible is a context."

"A page of history is worth a volume of logic," said Mr. Justice Oliver Wendell Holmes. Jesus and the apostles quoted the Old Testament prophecies in their historical sense, and it is evident throughout the New Testament that their hearers understood those prophecies in the same historical sense. An interpretation that changes this meaning is a distortion.

A proposition of fact is proved when its truth is established by competent and satisfactory evidence. By competent evidence is meant such evidence as the nature of the thing to be proved admits. By satisfactory evidence is meant that amount of proof which ordinarily satisfies an unprejudiced mind beyond reasonable doubt.

> Scripture facts are therefore proved when they are established by that kind and degree of evidence which would in the affairs of ordinary life satisfy the mind and conscience of a common man. When we have this kind and degree of evidence it is unreasonable to require more. (*Systematic Theology*, Augustus H. Strong, p. 142, Judson Press, 1899.)

A recent book with the title, *A Lawyer Among the Theologians*, stresses the need for established rules of interpretation and laws of evidence in biblical studies, which we have long advocated. The author is Norman Anderson who is director of the Institute of Advanced Legal Studies at the University of London and editor of *The World's Religions*.

In his book, Professor Anderson says it is astonishing to see how many biblical interpreters impose their preconceived ideas on the Scriptures rather than to evaluate the evidence as it stands. The fundamental problem of correct interpretation is to properly evaluate the evidence and to follow it to whatever conclusion it may lead us.

He deplores the method some interpreters use of quoting a passage which agrees with a thesis, and ignoring other passages which disagree with the interpreter's argument. Those who use "inspired guesswork" do not know the difference between fact and opinion.

The author also says that some theologians make dogmatic statements about points on which other competent authorities take a very different view and submit proofs for their beliefs, while the former do not. The proper evaluation of evidence is the basis of correct interpretation, legal or biblical. (Eerdmans Publishing Company, Grand Rapids, 1974, pp. 9-28.)

Notes

NOTES TO CHAPTER 2

1. Vine's *An Expository Dictionary of New Testament Words* (hereafter referred to as Vine's *Dictionary*) (Westwood, N.J.: Fleming H. Revell Co., 1948), 43:4.

2. *The International Standard Bible Encyclopaedia* (Grand Rapids: William B. Eerdmans Publishing Co., 1939), 4:2819.

3. Thayer's *A Greek-English Lexicon of the New Testament* (hereafter referred to as Thayer's *Lexicon*), p. 472.

4. Arndt and Gingrich's *A Greek-English Lexicon of the New Testament* (hereafter referred to as Arndt and Gingrich's *Lexicon*), p. 246; Vine's *Dictionary*, 2:40; Thayer's *Lexicon*, p. 200.

5. Moulton and Milligan's *The Vocabulary of the Greek New Testament*, p. 304 (hereafter referred to as Moulton and Milligan's *Vocabulary*).

6. Arndt and Gingrich's *Lexicon*, pp. 362-3; Thayer's *Lexicon*, p. 291.

NOTES TO CHAPTER 3

1. Thayer's *Lexicon*, p. 279.

2. Dana and Mantey's *A Manual Grammar of the Greek New Testament* (hereafter referred to as Dana and Mantey's *Grammar*), p. 244.

3. Vincent's *Word Studies in the New Testament* (hereafter referred to as Vincent's *Word Studies*), 4:45.

4. Vine's *Dictionary.*
5. Keil and Delitzsch's *Old Testament Commentaries.*

NOTES TO CHAPTER 4

1. See Alford's *The Greek New Testament for English Readers* (hereafter referred to as Alford's *New Testament*), p. 1332.
2. Hastings' *Dictionary of the Bible,* p. 820.
3. Richardson's *A Theological Word Book of the Bible,* p. 220.
4. Arndt and Gingrich's *Lexicon,* pp. 805-6.
5. Page 622.

NOTES TO CHAPTER 5

1. *The Pulpit Commentary.*
2. Alford's *New Testament.*
3. Jamieson, Fausset and Brown's commentary.
4. Girdlestone's *Synonyms of the Old Testament,* p. 295.
5. Vine's *Dictionary.*
6. Trench's *Synonyms of the New Testament,* p. 203.

NOTES TO CHAPTER 6

1. Headline in the Worldgram section of *U.S. News and World Report,* April 1, 1974, p. 55.

NOTES TO CHAPTER 7

1. Arndt and Gingrich's Lexicon, p. 678.

NOTES TO CHAPTER 8

1. Arndt and Gingrich's *Lexicon,* p. 77.
2. Moulton and Milligan's *Vocabulary,* p. 51.
3. Vine's *Dictionary,* 4:237.
4. Robertson's *Word Pictures in the New Testament* (hereafter referred to as Robertson's *Word Pictures*), 1:27.
5. Dana and Mantey's *Grammar,* p. 261.
6. Arndt and Gingrich's *Lexicon,* p. 646.
7. Robertson's *Word Pictures,* 6:153.
8. Alford's *New Testament,* p. 1674. Other Greek authorities support this interpretation. See especially the

Expositor's Greek Testament and *The New Testament from 26 Translations.*

9. Trench's *Synonyms of the New Testament*, p. 279.

NOTES TO CHAPTER 9

1. Arndt and Gingrich's *Lexicon*, p. xxvii.
2. Alford's *New Testament* (italics his), p. 1922.

NOTES TO CHAPTER 10

1. Edersheim's *The Life and Times of Jesus the Messiah*, 2:448.
2. *Ibid.*, 2:448 (footnote).
3. Schaff's *History of the Christian Church*, 1:186.
4. Robertson's *Word Pictures*, 2:262.
5. Gundry's *The Church and the Tribulation*, p. 92.
6. Bengel's *New Testament Word Studies*, 2:485.
7. Nestles' *Novum Testamentum Graece.*
8. Lamsa's *The New Testament According to the Eastern Text.*
9. Page 84.
10. Jamieson, Fausset and Brown's commentary.
11. Robertson's *Word Pictures*, 1:189.

NOTES TO CHAPTER 11

1. Bengel's *New Testament Word Studies*, 2:485.
2. *Theological Dictionary of the New Testament*, 6:30.
3. In addition to the three quoted examples, see also *The Pulpit Commentary*; Jamieson, Fausset and Brown's commentary; the *Expositor's Greek New Testament*; Vincent's *Word Studies*, and others.
4. Girdlestone's *The Grammar of Prophecy*, pp. 66, 179.
5. See 2:947-953; 3:139-146; 6:30.

Bibliography

Abbot, Lyman. *The Gospel According to Matthew,* "Interpretation." A. S. Barnes Co., 1878.

Abbot-Smith, G. A. *A Manual Greek Lexicon of the New Testament.* New York: Charles Scribner's Sons, undated.

Alford, Henry. *The Greek New Testament for English Readers.* Chicago: Moody Press, undated.

Amplified New Testament. Grand Rapids: Zondervan Publishing Co., 1958.

Anderson, Norman. *A Lawyer Among the Theologians.* Grand Rapids: William B. Eerdmans Publishing Company, 1974.

Arndt, Wm. F., and Gingrich, F. W. *A Greek-English Lexicon of the New Testament.* Chicago: University of Chicago Press, 1957.

Bengel, Johann A. *New Testament Word Studies.* Grand Rapids: Kregel Publications, 2 vols., reprint, 1971.

Berkhof, L. *Principles of Biblical Interpretation,* Grand Rapids: Baker Book House, 1960.

Black, H. C. *Black's Law Dictionary.* St. Paul: West Publishing Co., 1951.

Broom, Herbert. *Principles of Legal Interpretation.* London: Sweet & Maxwell, Ltd., 1937.

Burrows, Sir Roland. *Interpretation of Documents.* London: Butterworth & Co., 1946.

155

Cardoza, Benjamin. "The Nature of the Judicial Process," *The World of Law*, ed. Ephraim London. New York: Simon & Schuster, 2 vol., first printing, 1960.

Cremer, Hermann. *Biblico-Theological Lexicon of New Testament Greek*. Edinburgh: T. & T. Clark, reprint, 1954.

Dana, H. B., and Mantey, Julius B. *A Manual Grammar of the Greek New Testament*. New York: The Macmillan Co., 25th edition, 1960.

Deissmann, Adolph. *Light from the Ancient East*. Translated by Lionel R. M. Strachan. Grand Rapids: Baker Book House, reprint, 1965.

Edersheim, Alfred. *The Life and Times of Jesus the Messiah*. Grand Rapids: Wm. B. Eerdmans Co., V. 1, xii, xiii, 1953.

Encyclopedia Americana, "Interpretation." V. 15, p. 261 (1953), V. 15, p. 265 (1958).

Encyclopaedia Britannica, "Interpretation of Documents." V. 6, p. 615 (1952), V. 6, p. 265 (1958), V. 8, p. 912 (1959), V. 7, p. 514 (1965).

Expositors Greek New Testament. Grand Rapids: Wm. B. Eerdmans Co., 5 Vols., 1956.

Farrar, Frederic W. *History of Interpretation*. Grand Rapids: Baker Book House, 1961.

Finney, Charles G. *Autobiography*. Fleming H. Revell Co., undated.

Flesch, Rudolph. *How To Make Sense*. New York: Harper & Bros., 1954.

Girdlestone, R. B. *The Grammar of Prophecy*. Grand Rapids: Kregel Publications, 1955.

———. *Synonyms of the Old Testament—Their Bearing on Christian Doctrine*. Grand Rapids: Wm. B. Eerdmans Co., undated.

Gundry, Robert H. *The Church and the Tribulation*. Grand Rapids: Zondervan Publishing House, 1973.

Hastings, James, Ed. *Dictionary of the Bible*. New York: Charles Scribner's Sons, 1918.

Holmes, Oliver Wendell, Jr. "The Path of the Law," *The World of Law*. Ed. Ephraim London. New York: Simon & Schuster, V. 2, p. 630, 1960.

Inspiration and Interpretation. Grand Rapids: Wm. B. Eerdmans Co., 1957.

Interlinear Greek-English New Testament. The Nestle Greek Text with a Literal English Translation, by Alfred Marshall. London: Samuel Bagster and Sons Limited, 1967.

Jamieson, Fausset & Brown. *Commentary on the Whole Bible*. Grand Rapids: Wm. B. Eerdmans Co., 6 vols., 1945.

Josephus Historical Works, New and Complete Edition. Philadelphia: Henry T. Coates & Co., undated.

Keil & Delitzsch. *Old Testament Commentaries*. Grand Rapids: Associated Publishers and Authors, Inc., 6 vols., undated.

Kittel, G. and G. Friedrich. Editors. *Theological Dictionary of the New Testament*. Grand Rapids: Wm. B. Eerdmans Co., 9 vols., 1964.

Lamsa, George M. *The New Testament According to the Eastern Text*. Translated from Original Aramaic Sources. Philadelphia: A. J. Holman Company, 1940.

Marsh, F. E. *The Structural Principles of the Bible*. Grand Rapids: Kregel Publications, undated.

Moffat, James. *The Holy Bible*, A New Translation by James Moffat. New York: Harper & Brothers, 1926.

Moulton, James Hope, and Milligan, George. *The Vocabulary of the Greek New Testament*. Grand Rapids: Wm. B. Eerdmans Co., 1949.

Nestle, D. Eberhard and Nestle, D. Ervin. *Novum Testamentum Graece*. Privileg. Wurtt. Bibelanstalt Stuttgart, 1960.

Orr, James, Ed. *International Standard Bible Encyclopedia*. Grand Rapids: Wm. B. Eerdmans Co., 5 vols., 1952.

Pulpit Commentary. "Matthew," V. 1, xxv, old edition. New York: Funk & Wagnalls Co., 52 vols. undated.

Ramm, Bernard. *Protestant Biblical Interpretation*. Boston: W. A. Wilde Co., 1956.

Richardson, Alan, Ed. *Theological Word Book of the Bible*. New York: The Macmillan Co., seventh printing, 1958.

Robertson, A. T. *Word Pictures in the New Testament*.

Nashville: Broadman Press, ninth printing, 6 vols., 1933.

Schaff, Philip. *History of the Christian Church.* Grand Rapids: Associated Publishers and Authors, Inc., 3 vols., undated.

Strong, Augustus. *Systematic Theology.* Philadelphia: Judson Press, 1899.

Terry, M. S. *Biblical Hermeneutics.* New York: Hunt & Eaton, 1895.

Thayer, J. H. *A Greek-English Lexicon of the New Testament.* New York: American Book Company, 1889.

Toffler, Alvin. *Future Shock.* New York: Bantam Books, Inc., 1971.

Torrey, R. A. *The Importance and Value of Proper Bible Study.* Chicago: Moody Press, 1921.

Trench, R. C. *Synonyms of the New Testament.* Grand Rapids: Wm. B. Eerdmans Publishing Co., 1958.

Vaughan, Curtis. Ed. *New Testament from 26 Translations.* Grand Rapids: Zondervan Publishing Co., 1967.

Vincent, M. R. *Word Studies in the New Testament.* Grand Rapids: Wm. B. Eerdmans Publishing Co., 4 vols., 1957.

Vine, W. E. *An Expository Dictionary of New Testament Words.* London: Oliphants Ltd., 4 vols., 1948.

Walvoord, John F. Ed. *Inspiration and Interpretation.* Grand Rapids: Wm. B. Eerdmans Co., first printing, 1957.

Weymouth, R. F. *The New Testament in Modern Speech.* Boston: The Pilgrim Press. 1937.

Woodruff, Edwin H. *Introduction to the Study of Law.* New York: Baker, Voorhis & Company, 1898.

Wuest, Kenneth. *Studies in the Vocabulary of the Greek New Testament.* Grand Rapids: Wm. B. Eerdmans Publishing Co., 1945.

Young, Robert. *Analytical Concordance to the Bible.* Twentieth American edition. New York: Funk & Wagnalls Co., undated.